This Cheese Journal Belongs To:

_____

DEDICATION

This Cheese Tasting Journal Log book is dedicated to all the cheese lovers out there who love to try & review different cheeses and document their findings in the process.

You are my inspiration for producing books and I'm honored to be a part of keeping all of your Cheese notes and records organized.

This journal notebook will help you record your details about tasting new cheeses.

Thoughtfully put together with these sections to record:

Name of Cheese, Factory, Origin, Date & Price, Rind, Flavors, Milk, Texture Meter, Rating, and Notes.

HOW TO USE THIS BOOK

The purpose of this book is to keep all of your Cheese Tasting notes all in one place. It will help keep you organized.

This Cheese Tasting Journal will allow you to accurately document every detail about trying new Cheeses. It's a great way to chart your course through tasting cheeses.

Here are examples of the prompts for you to fill in and write about your experience in this book:

1. **Name Of Cheese** - Log the name of the cheese you are reviewing or recording.
2. **Factory** - Which factory you purchased from.
3. **Origin, Date & Price** - Write & mark where the cheese came from, the day, date and price you bought it for.
4. **Rind** - (Bloomy, White, Soft, Fuzzy, Washed, Salty, Natural, Thick, Hard, Gritty, Dry) - with check mark boxes
5. **Flavors** - (Salty, Sweet, Crystalline, Crumbly, Sharp/ Tangy, Milky/ Lactic, Lemon, Buttery/ Creamy, Grassy, Robust, Herbal, Skinky, Caramel, Moldy/ Blue, Nutty, Earthy).
6. **Milk** - (Cow, Sheep, Goat, Raw, Other).
7. **Texture Meter** - (Runny, Soft, Semi-Soft, Semi-Firm, Firm, Hard).
8. **Rating** - Rate your experience with 1-5 stars.
9. **Notes** - Blank lined space for writing any important information you like, for example if you tasted your cheese with milk, wine or beer, any ideas for eating new cheeses you may find, what inspired you, what you enjoy, which one you really liked & love, any thoughts, what type is your favorite, etc.

NAME OF CHEESE _____

FACTORY _____

RIND

- ☐ BLOOMY ☐ WASHED ☐ NATURAL ☐ DRY
  - ☐ WHITE   ☐ SALTY   ☐ THICK
  - ☐ SOFT   ☐ HARD
  - ☐ FUZZY   ☐ GRITTY

ORIGIN _____

DATE _____

PRICE _____

FLAVORS

- ☐ SALTY
- ☐ SWEET
- ☐ CRYSTALLINE
- ☐ CRUMBLY
- ☐ SHARP/TANGY
- ☐ MILKY/LACTIC
- ☐ LEMON
- ☐ BUTTERY/CREAMY
- ☐ GRASSY
- ☐ ROBUST
- ☐ HERBAL
- ☐ SKINKY
- ☐ CARAMEL
- ☐ MOLDY/BLUE
- ☐ NUTTY
- ☐ EARTHY

MILK

- ☐ COW
- ☐ SHEEP
- ☐ GOAT
- ☐ RAW
- ☐ OTHER: _____
  _____
  _____

TEXTURE METER

- RUNNY
- SOFT
- SEMI-SOFT
- SEMI-FIRM
- FIRM
- HARD

NOTES

_____
_____
_____
_____
_____
_____

RATING

☆☆☆☆☆

NAME OF CHEESE _____

FACTORY _____

RIND

- [ ] BLOOMY [ ] WASHED [ ] NATURAL [ ] DRY
  - [ ] WHITE [ ] SALTY [ ] THICK
  - [ ] SOFT   [ ] HARD
  - [ ] FUZZY   [ ] GRITTY

ORIGIN _____

DATE _____

PRICE _____

FLAVORS

- [ ] SALTY
- [ ] SWEET
- [ ] CRYSTALLINE
- [ ] CRUMBLY
- [ ] SHARP/TANGY
- [ ] MILKY/LACTIC
- [ ] LEMON
- [ ] BUTTERY/CREAMY
- [ ] GRASSY
- [ ] ROBUST
- [ ] HERBAL
- [ ] SKINKY
- [ ] CARAMEL
- [ ] MOLDY/BLUE
- [ ] NUTTY
- [ ] EARTHY

MILK

- [ ] COW
- [ ] SHEEP
- [ ] GOAT
- [ ] RAW
- [ ] OTHER: _____
  _____
  _____

TEXTURE METER

- RUNNY
- SOFT
- SEMI-SOFT
- SEMI-FIRM
- FIRM
- HARD

NOTES

_____
_____
_____
_____
_____
_____
_____

RATING

☆☆☆☆☆

NAME OF CHEESE _____

FACTORY _____

RIND
- ☐ BLOOMY ☐ WASHED ☐ NATURAL ☐ DRY
  - ☐ WHITE   ☐ SALTY   ☐ THICK
  - ☐ SOFT   ☐ HARD
  - ☐ FUZZY   ☐ GRITTY

ORIGIN _____

DATE _____

PRICE _____

FLAVORS
- ☐ SALTY   ☐ GRASSY
- ☐ SWEET   ☐ ROBUST
- ☐ CRYSTALLINE   ☐ HERBAL
- ☐ CRUMBLY   ☐ SKINKY
- ☐ SHARP/TANGY   ☐ CARAMEL
- ☐ MILKY/LACTIC   ☐ MOLDY/BLUE
- ☐ LEMON   ☐ NUTTY
- ☐ BUTTERY/CREAMY ☐ EARTHY

MILK
- ☐ COW
- ☐ SHEEP
- ☐ GOAT
- ☐ RAW
- ☐ OTHER: _____
  _____
  _____

TEXTURE METER
- RUNNY
- SOFT
- SEMI-SOFT
- SEMI-FIRM
- FIRM
- HARD

NOTES
_____
_____
_____
_____
_____

RATING
☆ ☆ ☆ ☆ ☆

NAME OF CHEESE _____

FACTORY _____

RIND
- ☐ BLOOMY   ☐ WASHED   ☐ NATURAL   ☐ DRY
  - ☐ WHITE   ☐ SALTY   ☐ THICK
  - ☐ SOFT   ☐ HARD
  - ☐ FUZZY   ☐ GRITTY

ORIGIN _____

DATE _____

PRICE _____

FLAVORS
- ☐ SALTY   ☐ GRASSY
- ☐ SWEET   ☐ ROBUST
- ☐ CRYSTALLINE   ☐ HERBAL
- ☐ CRUMBLY   ☐ SKINKY
- ☐ SHARP/TANGY   ☐ CARAMEL
- ☐ MILKY/LACTIC   ☐ MOLDY/BLUE
- ☐ LEMON   ☐ NUTTY
- ☐ BUTTERY/CREAMY ☐ EARTHY

MILK
- ☐ COW
- ☐ SHEEP
- ☐ GOAT
- ☐ RAW
- ☐ OTHER: _____
  _____
  _____

TEXTURE METER
- RUNNY
- SOFT
- SEMI-SOFT
- SEMI-FIRM
- FIRM
- HARD

NOTES
_____
_____
_____
_____
_____
_____

RATING
☆ ☆ ☆ ☆ ☆

NAME OF CHEESE _____

FACTORY _____

RIND
- ☐ BLOOMY ☐ WASHED ☐ NATURAL ☐ DRY
  - ☐ WHITE ☐ SALTY ☐ THICK
  - ☐ SOFT ☐ HARD
  - ☐ FUZZY ☐ GRITTY

ORIGIN _____

DATE _____

PRICE _____

FLAVORS
- ☐ SALTY
- ☐ SWEET
- ☐ CRYSTALLINE
- ☐ CRUMBLY
- ☐ SHARP/TANGY
- ☐ MILKY/LACTIC
- ☐ LEMON
- ☐ BUTTERY/CREAMY
- ☐ GRASSY
- ☐ ROBUST
- ☐ HERBAL
- ☐ SKINKY
- ☐ CARAMEL
- ☐ MOLDY/BLUE
- ☐ NUTTY
- ☐ EARTHY

MILK
- ☐ COW
- ☐ SHEEP
- ☐ GOAT
- ☐ RAW
- ☐ OTHER: _____

TEXTURE METER
- RUNNY
- SOFT
- SEMI-SOFT
- SEMI-FIRM
- FIRM
- HARD

NOTES
_____
_____
_____
_____
_____
_____

RATING
☆☆☆☆☆

NAME OF CHEESE _____

FACTORY _____

RIND
- [ ] BLOOMY
- [ ] WASHED
- [ ] NATURAL
- [ ] DRY
  - [ ] WHITE
  - [ ] SALTY
  - [ ] THICK
  - [ ] SOFT
  - [ ] HARD
  - [ ] FUZZY
  - [ ] GRITTY

ORIGIN _____

DATE _____

PRICE _____

FLAVORS
- [ ] SALTY
- [ ] GRASSY
- [ ] SWEET
- [ ] ROBUST
- [ ] CRYSTALLINE
- [ ] HERBAL
- [ ] CRUMBLY
- [ ] SKINKY
- [ ] SHARP/TANGY
- [ ] CARAMEL
- [ ] MILKY/LACTIC
- [ ] MOLDY/BLUE
- [ ] LEMON
- [ ] NUTTY
- [ ] BUTTERY/CREAMY
- [ ] EARTHY

MILK
- [ ] COW
- [ ] SHEEP
- [ ] GOAT
- [ ] RAW
- [ ] OTHER: _____

TEXTURE METER
- RUNNY
- SOFT
- SEMI-SOFT
- SEMI-FIRM
- FIRM
- HARD

NOTES
_____
_____
_____
_____
_____
_____

RATING ☆☆☆☆☆

NAME OF CHEESE _____

FACTORY _____

RIND

- ☐ BLOOMY ☐ WASHED ☐ NATURAL ☐ DRY
  - ☐ WHITE ☐ SALTY ☐ THICK
  - ☐ SOFT   ☐ HARD
  - ☐ FUZZY   ☐ GRITTY

ORIGIN _____

DATE _____

PRICE _____

FLAVORS

- ☐ SALTY
- ☐ SWEET
- ☐ CRYSTALLINE
- ☐ CRUMBLY
- ☐ SHARP/TANGY
- ☐ MILKY/LACTIC
- ☐ LEMON
- ☐ BUTTERY/CREAMY
- ☐ GRASSY
- ☐ ROBUST
- ☐ HERBAL
- ☐ SKINKY
- ☐ CARAMEL
- ☐ MOLDY/BLUE
- ☐ NUTTY
- ☐ EARTHY

MILK

- ☐ COW
- ☐ SHEEP
- ☐ GOAT
- ☐ RAW
- ☐ OTHER: _____
  _____
  _____

TEXTURE METER

- RUNNY
- SOFT
- SEMI-SOFT
- SEMI-FIRM
- FIRM
- HARD

NOTES

_____
_____
_____
_____
_____

RATING ☆☆☆☆☆

NAME OF CHEESE _____

FACTORY _____

RIND

- ☐ BLOOMY ☐ WASHED ☐ NATURAL ☐ DRY
  - ☐ WHITE ☐ SALTY ☐ THICK
  - ☐ SOFT ☐ HARD
  - ☐ FUZZY ☐ GRITTY

ORIGIN _____

DATE _____

PRICE _____

FLAVORS

- ☐ SALTY
- ☐ SWEET
- ☐ CRYSTALLINE
- ☐ CRUMBLY
- ☐ SHARP/TANGY
- ☐ MILKY/LACTIC
- ☐ LEMON
- ☐ BUTTERY/CREAMY
- ☐ GRASSY
- ☐ ROBUST
- ☐ HERBAL
- ☐ SKINKY
- ☐ CARAMEL
- ☐ MOLDY/BLUE
- ☐ NUTTY
- ☐ EARTHY

MILK

- ☐ COW
- ☐ SHEEP
- ☐ GOAT
- ☐ RAW
- ☐ OTHER: _____
  _____
  _____

TEXTURE METER

- RUNNY
- SOFT
- SEMI-SOFT
- SEMI-FIRM
- FIRM
- HARD

NOTES

_____
_____
_____
_____
_____
_____

RATING

☆☆☆☆☆

NAME OF CHEESE _____

FACTORY _____

RIND

- [ ] BLOOMY
- [ ] WASHED
- [ ] NATURAL
- [ ] DRY
  - [ ] WHITE
  - [ ] SALTY
  - [ ] THICK
  - [ ] SOFT
  - [ ] HARD
  - [ ] FUZZY
  - [ ] GRITTY

ORIGIN _____

DATE _____

PRICE _____

FLAVORS

- [ ] SALTY
- [ ] GRASSY
- [ ] SWEET
- [ ] ROBUST
- [ ] CRYSTALLINE
- [ ] HERBAL
- [ ] CRUMBLY
- [ ] SKINKY
- [ ] SHARP/TANGY
- [ ] CARAMEL
- [ ] MILKY/LACTIC
- [ ] MOLDY/BLUE
- [ ] LEMON
- [ ] NUTTY
- [ ] BUTTERY/CREAMY
- [ ] EARTHY

MILK

- [ ] COW
- [ ] SHEEP
- [ ] GOAT
- [ ] RAW
- [ ] OTHER: _____

TEXTURE METER

- RUNNY
- SOFT
- SEMI-SOFT
- SEMI-FIRM
- FIRM
- HARD

NOTES

_____
_____
_____
_____
_____
_____

RATING

☆☆☆☆☆

NAME OF CHEESE _____

FACTORY _____

RIND

- [ ] BLOOMY [ ] WASHED [ ] NATURAL [ ] DRY
  - [ ] WHITE [ ] SALTY [ ] THICK
  - [ ] SOFT   [ ] HARD
  - [ ] FUZZY [ ] GRITTY

ORIGIN _____

DATE _____

PRICE _____

FLAVORS

- [ ] SALTY
- [ ] SWEET
- [ ] CRYSTALLINE
- [ ] CRUMBLY
- [ ] SHARP/TANGY
- [ ] MILKY/LACTIC
- [ ] LEMON
- [ ] BUTTERY/CREAMY
- [ ] GRASSY
- [ ] ROBUST
- [ ] HERBAL
- [ ] SKINKY
- [ ] CARAMEL
- [ ] MOLDY/BLUE
- [ ] NUTTY
- [ ] EARTHY

MILK

- [ ] COW
- [ ] SHEEP
- [ ] GOAT
- [ ] RAW
- [ ] OTHER: _____
  _____
  _____

TEXTURE METER

- RUNNY
- SOFT
- SEMI-SOFT
- SEMI-FIRM
- FIRM
- HARD

NOTES

_____
_____
_____
_____
_____
_____
_____

RATING
☆ ☆ ☆ ☆ ☆

NAME OF CHEESE _____

FACTORY _____

RIND
- [ ] BLOOMY
- [ ] WASHED
- [ ] NATURAL
- [ ] DRY
  - [ ] WHITE
  - [ ] SALTY
  - [ ] THICK
  - [ ] SOFT
  - [ ] HARD
  - [ ] FUZZY
  - [ ] GRITTY

ORIGIN _____

DATE _____

PRICE _____

FLAVORS
- [ ] SALTY
- [ ] GRASSY
- [ ] SWEET
- [ ] ROBUST
- [ ] CRYSTALLINE
- [ ] HERBAL
- [ ] CRUMBLY
- [ ] SKINKY
- [ ] SHARP/TANGY
- [ ] CARAMEL
- [ ] MILKY/LACTIC
- [ ] MOLDY/BLUE
- [ ] LEMON
- [ ] NUTTY
- [ ] BUTTERY/CREAMY
- [ ] EARTHY

MILK
- [ ] COW
- [ ] SHEEP
- [ ] GOAT
- [ ] RAW
- [ ] OTHER: _____
  _____
  _____

TEXTURE METER
- RUNNY
- SOFT
- SEMI-SOFT
- SEMI-FIRM
- FIRM
- HARD

NOTES
_____
_____
_____
_____
_____
_____

RATING
☆☆☆☆☆

NAME OF CHEESE _____

FACTORY _____

RIND

- [ ] BLOOMY
- [ ] WASHED
- [ ] NATURAL
- [ ] DRY
  - [ ] WHITE
  - [ ] SALTY
  - [ ] THICK
  - [ ] SOFT
  - [ ] HARD
  - [ ] FUZZY
  - [ ] GRITTY

ORIGIN _____

DATE _____

PRICE _____

FLAVORS

- [ ] SALTY
- [ ] SWEET
- [ ] CRYSTALLINE
- [ ] CRUMBLY
- [ ] SHARP/TANGY
- [ ] MILKY/LACTIC
- [ ] LEMON
- [ ] BUTTERY/CREAMY
- [ ] GRASSY
- [ ] ROBUST
- [ ] HERBAL
- [ ] SKINKY
- [ ] CARAMEL
- [ ] MOLDY/BLUE
- [ ] NUTTY
- [ ] EARTHY

MILK

- [ ] COW
- [ ] SHEEP
- [ ] GOAT
- [ ] RAW
- [ ] OTHER:
  _____
  _____
  _____

TEXTURE METER

- RUNNY
- SOFT
- SEMI-SOFT
- SEMI-FIRM
- FIRM
- HARD

NOTES

_____
_____
_____
_____
_____
_____

RATING

☆☆☆☆☆

NAME OF CHEESE _____

FACTORY _____

RIND
- ☐ BLOOMY ☐ WASHED ☐ NATURAL ☐ DRY
  - ☐ WHITE ☐ SALTY ☐ THICK
  - ☐ SOFT ☐ HARD
  - ☐ FUZZY ☐ GRITTY

ORIGIN _____

DATE _____

PRICE _____

FLAVORS
- ☐ SALTY
- ☐ SWEET
- ☐ CRYSTALLINE
- ☐ CRUMBLY
- ☐ SHARP/TANGY
- ☐ MILKY/LACTIC
- ☐ LEMON
- ☐ BUTTERY/CREAMY
- ☐ GRASSY
- ☐ ROBUST
- ☐ HERBAL
- ☐ SKINKY
- ☐ CARAMEL
- ☐ MOLDY/BLUE
- ☐ NUTTY
- ☐ EARTHY

MILK
- ☐ COW
- ☐ SHEEP
- ☐ GOAT
- ☐ RAW
- ☐ OTHER: _____

TEXTURE METER
- RUNNY
- SOFT
- SEMI-SOFT
- SEMI-FIRM
- FIRM
- HARD

NOTES
_____
_____
_____
_____
_____
_____

RATING ☆☆☆☆☆

NAME OF CHEESE _____

FACTORY _____

RIND
- [ ] BLOOMY
- [ ] WASHED
- [ ] NATURAL
- [ ] DRY
  - [ ] WHITE
  - [ ] SALTY
  - [ ] THICK
  - [ ] SOFT
  - [ ] HARD
  - [ ] FUZZY
  - [ ] GRITTY

ORIGIN _____

DATE _____

PRICE _____

FLAVORS
- [ ] SALTY
- [ ] SWEET
- [ ] CRYSTALLINE
- [ ] CRUMBLY
- [ ] SHARP/TANGY
- [ ] MILKY/LACTIC
- [ ] LEMON
- [ ] BUTTERY/CREAMY
- [ ] GRASSY
- [ ] ROBUST
- [ ] HERBAL
- [ ] SKINKY
- [ ] CARAMEL
- [ ] MOLDY/BLUE
- [ ] NUTTY
- [ ] EARTHY

MILK
- [ ] COW
- [ ] SHEEP
- [ ] GOAT
- [ ] RAW
- [ ] OTHER: _____

TEXTURE METER
- RUNNY
- SOFT
- SEMI-SOFT
- SEMI-FIRM
- FIRM
- HARD

NOTES
_____
_____
_____
_____
_____
_____

RATING ☆☆☆☆☆

NAME OF CHEESE _____

FACTORY _____

RIND
☐ BLOOMY ☐ WASHED ☐ NATURAL ☐ DRY
☐ WHITE   ☐ SALTY   ☐ THICK
☐ SOFT   ☐ HARD
☐ FUZZY   ☐ GRITTY

ORIGIN _____

DATE _____

PRICE _____

FLAVORS		MILK	TEXTURE METER
☐ SALTY	☐ GRASSY	☐ COW	RUNNY
☐ SWEET	☐ ROBUST	☐ SHEEP	SOFT
☐ CRYSTALLINE	☐ HERBAL	☐ GOAT	SEMI-SOFT
☐ CRUMBLY	☐ SKINKY	☐ RAW	SEMI-FIRM
☐ SHARP/TANGY	☐ CARAMEL	☐ OTHER:	FIRM
☐ MILKY/LACTIC	☐ MOLDY/BLUE	_____	HARD
☐ LEMON	☐ NUTTY	_____	
☐ BUTTERY/CREAMY	☐ EARTHY	_____	

NOTES

_____

_____

_____

_____

_____

_____

RATING
☆☆☆☆☆

NAME OF CHEESE _____

FACTORY _____

RIND
- [ ] BLOOMY [ ] WASHED [ ] NATURAL [ ] DRY
  - [ ] WHITE   [ ] SALTY   [ ] THICK
  - [ ] SOFT   [ ] HARD
  - [ ] FUZZY   [ ] GRITTY

ORIGIN _____

DATE _____

PRICE _____

FLAVORS
- [ ] SALTY
- [ ] SWEET
- [ ] CRYSTALLINE
- [ ] CRUMBLY
- [ ] SHARP/TANGY
- [ ] MILKY/LACTIC
- [ ] LEMON
- [ ] BUTTERY/CREAMY
- [ ] GRASSY
- [ ] ROBUST
- [ ] HERBAL
- [ ] SKINKY
- [ ] CARAMEL
- [ ] MOLDY/BLUE
- [ ] NUTTY
- [ ] EARTHY

MILK
- [ ] COW
- [ ] SHEEP
- [ ] GOAT
- [ ] RAW
- [ ] OTHER: _____
  _____
  _____

TEXTURE METER
- RUNNY
- SOFT
- SEMI-SOFT
- SEMI-FIRM
- FIRM
- HARD

NOTES
_____
_____
_____
_____
_____
_____

RATING
☆☆☆☆☆

NAME OF CHEESE _____

FACTORY _____

RIND
- ☐ BLOOMY ☐ WASHED ☐ NATURAL ☐ DRY
  - ☐ WHITE ☐ SALTY ☐ THICK
  - ☐ SOFT ☐ HARD
  - ☐ FUZZY ☐ GRITTY

ORIGIN _____

DATE _____

PRICE _____

FLAVORS
- ☐ SALTY ☐ GRASSY
- ☐ SWEET ☐ ROBUST
- ☐ CRYSTALLINE ☐ HERBAL
- ☐ CRUMBLY ☐ SKINKY
- ☐ SHARP/TANGY ☐ CARAMEL
- ☐ MILKY/LACTIC ☐ MOLDY/BLUE
- ☐ LEMON ☐ NUTTY
- ☐ BUTTERY/CREAMY ☐ EARTHY

MILK
- ☐ COW
- ☐ SHEEP
- ☐ GOAT
- ☐ RAW
- ☐ OTHER: _____
  _____
  _____

TEXTURE METER
- RUNNY
- SOFT
- SEMI-SOFT
- SEMI-FIRM
- FIRM
- HARD

NOTES
_____
_____
_____
_____
_____
_____

RATING
☆☆☆☆☆

NAME OF CHEESE _____

FACTORY _____

RIND
- [ ] BLOOMY
- [ ] WASHED
- [ ] NATURAL
- [ ] DRY
  - [ ] WHITE
  - [ ] SALTY
  - [ ] THICK
  - [ ] SOFT
  - [ ] HARD
  - [ ] FUZZY
  - [ ] GRITTY

ORIGIN _____

DATE _____

PRICE _____

FLAVORS
- [ ] SALTY
- [ ] GRASSY
- [ ] SWEET
- [ ] ROBUST
- [ ] CRYSTALLINE
- [ ] HERBAL
- [ ] CRUMBLY
- [ ] SKINKY
- [ ] SHARP/TANGY
- [ ] CARAMEL
- [ ] MILKY/LACTIC
- [ ] MOLDY/BLUE
- [ ] LEMON
- [ ] NUTTY
- [ ] BUTTERY/CREAMY
- [ ] EARTHY

MILK
- [ ] COW
- [ ] SHEEP
- [ ] GOAT
- [ ] RAW
- [ ] OTHER: _____
  _____
  _____

TEXTURE METER
- RUNNY
- SOFT
- SEMI-SOFT
- SEMI-FIRM
- FIRM
- HARD

NOTES
_____
_____
_____
_____
_____
_____

RATING
☆☆☆☆☆

NAME OF CHEESE _____

FACTORY _____

RIND
- ☐ BLOOMY ☐ WASHED ☐ NATURAL ☐ DRY
  - ☐ WHITE ☐ SALTY ☐ THICK
  - ☐ SOFT   ☐ HARD
  - ☐ FUZZY   ☐ GRITTY

ORIGIN _____

DATE _____

PRICE _____

FLAVORS
- ☐ SALTY
- ☐ SWEET
- ☐ CRYSTALLINE
- ☐ CRUMBLY
- ☐ SHARP/TANGY
- ☐ MILKY/LACTIC
- ☐ LEMON
- ☐ BUTTERY/CREAMY
- ☐ GRASSY
- ☐ ROBUST
- ☐ HERBAL
- ☐ SKINKY
- ☐ CARAMEL
- ☐ MOLDY/BLUE
- ☐ NUTTY
- ☐ EARTHY

MILK
- ☐ COW
- ☐ SHEEP
- ☐ GOAT
- ☐ RAW
- ☐ OTHER: _____
  _____
  _____

TEXTURE METER
- RUNNY
- SOFT
- SEMI-SOFT
- SEMI-FIRM
- FIRM
- HARD

NOTES
_____
_____
_____
_____
_____

RATING
☆ ☆ ☆ ☆ ☆

NAME OF CHEESE _____

FACTORY _____

RIND
- ☐ BLOOMY
- ☐ WASHED
- ☐ NATURAL
- ☐ DRY
  - ☐ WHITE
  - ☐ SALTY
  - ☐ THICK
  - ☐ SOFT
  - ☐ HARD
  - ☐ FUZZY
  - ☐ GRITTY

ORIGIN _____

DATE _____

PRICE _____

FLAVORS
- ☐ SALTY
- ☐ SWEET
- ☐ CRYSTALLINE
- ☐ CRUMBLY
- ☐ SHARP/TANGY
- ☐ MILKY/LACTIC
- ☐ LEMON
- ☐ BUTTERY/CREAMY
- ☐ GRASSY
- ☐ ROBUST
- ☐ HERBAL
- ☐ SKINKY
- ☐ CARAMEL
- ☐ MOLDY/BLUE
- ☐ NUTTY
- ☐ EARTHY

MILK
- ☐ COW
- ☐ SHEEP
- ☐ GOAT
- ☐ RAW
- ☐ OTHER: _____
  _____
  _____

TEXTURE METER
- RUNNY
- SOFT
- SEMI-SOFT
- SEMI-FIRM
- FIRM
- HARD

NOTES
_____
_____
_____
_____
_____
_____

RATING ☆☆☆☆☆

NAME OF CHEESE _____

FACTORY _____

RIND
- ☐ BLOOMY   ☐ WASHED   ☐ NATURAL   ☐ DRY
  - ☐ WHITE   ☐ SALTY   ☐ THICK
  - ☐ SOFT   ☐ HARD
  - ☐ FUZZY   ☐ GRITTY

ORIGIN _____

DATE _____

PRICE _____

FLAVORS
- ☐ SALTY
- ☐ SWEET
- ☐ CRYSTALLINE
- ☐ CRUMBLY
- ☐ SHARP/TANGY
- ☐ MILKY/LACTIC
- ☐ LEMON
- ☐ BUTTERY/CREAMY
- ☐ GRASSY
- ☐ ROBUST
- ☐ HERBAL
- ☐ SKINKY
- ☐ CARAMEL
- ☐ MOLDY/BLUE
- ☐ NUTTY
- ☐ EARTHY

MILK
- ☐ COW
- ☐ SHEEP
- ☐ GOAT
- ☐ RAW
- ☐ OTHER: _____
  _____
  _____

TEXTURE METER
- RUNNY
- SOFT
- SEMI-SOFT
- SEMI-FIRM
- FIRM
- HARD

NOTES
_____
_____
_____
_____
_____
_____

RATING ☆☆☆☆☆

NAME OF CHEESE _____

FACTORY _____

RIND
- [ ] BLOOMY
- [ ] WASHED
- [ ] NATURAL
- [ ] DRY
  - [ ] WHITE
  - [ ] SALTY
  - [ ] THICK
  - [ ] SOFT
  - [ ] HARD
  - [ ] FUZZY
  - [ ] GRITTY

ORIGIN _____

DATE _____

PRICE _____

FLAVORS
- [ ] SALTY
- [ ] SWEET
- [ ] CRYSTALLINE
- [ ] CRUMBLY
- [ ] SHARP/TANGY
- [ ] MILKY/LACTIC
- [ ] LEMON
- [ ] BUTTERY/CREAMY
- [ ] GRASSY
- [ ] ROBUST
- [ ] HERBAL
- [ ] SKINKY
- [ ] CARAMEL
- [ ] MOLDY/BLUE
- [ ] NUTTY
- [ ] EARTHY

MILK
- [ ] COW
- [ ] SHEEP
- [ ] GOAT
- [ ] RAW
- [ ] OTHER: _____

TEXTURE METER
- RUNNY
- SOFT
- SEMI-SOFT
- SEMI-FIRM
- FIRM
- HARD

NOTES
_____
_____
_____
_____
_____
_____

RATING ☆☆☆☆☆

NAME OF CHEESE _____

FACTORY _____

RIND
☐ BLOOMY ☐ WASHED ☐ NATURAL ☐ DRY
☐ WHITE   ☐ SALTY   ☐ THICK
☐ SOFT   ☐ HARD
☐ FUZZY   ☐ GRITTY

ORIGIN _____

DATE _____

PRICE _____

FLAVORS		MILK	TEXTURE METER
☐ SALTY	☐ GRASSY	☐ COW	RUNNY
☐ SWEET	☐ ROBUST	☐ SHEEP	SOFT
☐ CRYSTALLINE	☐ HERBAL	☐ GOAT	SEMI-SOFT
☐ CRUMBLY	☐ SKINKY	☐ RAW	SEMI-FIRM
☐ SHARP/TANGY	☐ CARAMEL	☐ OTHER:	FIRM
☐ MILKY/LACTIC	☐ MOLDY/BLUE	_____	HARD
☐ LEMON	☐ NUTTY	_____	
☐ BUTTERY/CREAMY	☐ EARTHY	_____	

NOTES

_____
_____
_____
_____
_____
_____

RATING
☆☆☆☆☆

NAME OF CHEESE _____

FACTORY _____

RIND

- [ ] BLOOMY
- [ ] WASHED
- [ ] NATURAL
- [ ] DRY
  - [ ] WHITE
  - [ ] SALTY
  - [ ] THICK
  - [ ] SOFT
  - [ ] HARD
  - [ ] FUZZY
  - [ ] GRITTY

ORIGIN _____

DATE _____

PRICE _____

FLAVORS

- [ ] SALTY
- [ ] GRASSY
- [ ] SWEET
- [ ] ROBUST
- [ ] CRYSTALLINE
- [ ] HERBAL
- [ ] CRUMBLY
- [ ] SKINKY
- [ ] SHARP/TANGY
- [ ] CARAMEL
- [ ] MILKY/LACTIC
- [ ] MOLDY/BLUE
- [ ] LEMON
- [ ] NUTTY
- [ ] BUTTERY/CREAMY
- [ ] EARTHY

MILK

- [ ] COW
- [ ] SHEEP
- [ ] GOAT
- [ ] RAW
- [ ] OTHER: _____

TEXTURE METER

- RUNNY
- SOFT
- SEMI-SOFT
- SEMI-FIRM
- FIRM
- HARD

NOTES

_____

RATING

☆☆☆☆☆

NAME OF CHEESE _____

FACTORY _____

RIND
- ☐ BLOOMY ☐ WASHED ☐ NATURAL ☐ DRY
  - ☐ WHITE ☐ SALTY ☐ THICK
  - ☐ SOFT   ☐ HARD
  - ☐ FUZZY ☐ GRITTY

ORIGIN _____

DATE _____

PRICE _____

FLAVORS
- ☐ SALTY   ☐ GRASSY
- ☐ SWEET   ☐ ROBUST
- ☐ CRYSTALLINE   ☐ HERBAL
- ☐ CRUMBLY   ☐ SKINKY
- ☐ SHARP/TANGY   ☐ CARAMEL
- ☐ MILKY/LACTIC   ☐ MOLDY/BLUE
- ☐ LEMON   ☐ NUTTY
- ☐ BUTTERY/CREAMY   ☐ EARTHY

MILK
- ☐ COW
- ☐ SHEEP
- ☐ GOAT
- ☐ RAW
- ☐ OTHER: _____
  _____
  _____

TEXTURE METER
- RUNNY
- SOFT
- SEMI-SOFT
- SEMI-FIRM
- FIRM
- HARD

NOTES
_____
_____
_____
_____
_____

RATING ☆☆☆☆☆

NAME OF CHEESE _____

FACTORY _____

RIND
- [ ] BLOOMY [ ] WASHED [ ] NATURAL [ ] DRY
  - [ ] WHITE   [ ] SALTY   [ ] THICK
  - [ ] SOFT   [ ] HARD
  - [ ] FUZZY   [ ] GRITTY

ORIGIN _____

DATE _____

PRICE _____

FLAVORS
- [ ] SALTY
- [ ] SWEET
- [ ] CRYSTALLINE
- [ ] CRUMBLY
- [ ] SHARP/TANGY
- [ ] MILKY/LACTIC
- [ ] LEMON
- [ ] BUTTERY/CREAMY
- [ ] GRASSY
- [ ] ROBUST
- [ ] HERBAL
- [ ] SKINKY
- [ ] CARAMEL
- [ ] MOLDY/BLUE
- [ ] NUTTY
- [ ] EARTHY

MILK
- [ ] COW
- [ ] SHEEP
- [ ] GOAT
- [ ] RAW
- [ ] OTHER: _____
  _____
  _____

TEXTURE METER
- RUNNY
- SOFT
- SEMI-SOFT
- SEMI-FIRM
- FIRM
- HARD

NOTES
_____
_____
_____
_____
_____
_____

RATING
☆ ☆ ☆ ☆ ☆

NAME OF CHEESE _____

FACTORY _____

RIND
- ☐ BLOOMY ☐ WASHED ☐ NATURAL ☐ DRY
  - ☐ WHITE ☐ SALTY ☐ THICK
  - ☐ SOFT ☐ HARD
  - ☐ FUZZY ☐ GRITTY

ORIGIN _____

DATE _____

PRICE _____

FLAVORS
- ☐ SALTY
- ☐ SWEET
- ☐ CRYSTALLINE
- ☐ CRUMBLY
- ☐ SHARP/TANGY
- ☐ MILKY/LACTIC
- ☐ LEMON
- ☐ BUTTERY/CREAMY
- ☐ GRASSY
- ☐ ROBUST
- ☐ HERBAL
- ☐ SKINKY
- ☐ CARAMEL
- ☐ MOLDY/BLUE
- ☐ NUTTY
- ☐ EARTHY

MILK
- ☐ COW
- ☐ SHEEP
- ☐ GOAT
- ☐ RAW
- ☐ OTHER: _____
  _____
  _____

TEXTURE METER
- RUNNY
- SOFT
- SEMI-SOFT
- SEMI-FIRM
- FIRM
- HARD

NOTES
_____
_____
_____
_____
_____
_____

RATING
☆ ☆ ☆ ☆ ☆

NAME OF CHEESE _____

FACTORY _____

RIND
- ☐ BLOOMY
- ☐ WASHED
- ☐ NATURAL
- ☐ DRY
  - ☐ WHITE
  - ☐ SALTY
  - ☐ THICK
  - ☐ SOFT
  - ☐ HARD
  - ☐ FUZZY
  - ☐ GRITTY

ORIGIN _____

DATE _____

PRICE _____

FLAVORS
- ☐ SALTY
- ☐ SWEET
- ☐ CRYSTALLINE
- ☐ CRUMBLY
- ☐ SHARP/TANGY
- ☐ MILKY/LACTIC
- ☐ LEMON
- ☐ BUTTERY/CREAMY
- ☐ GRASSY
- ☐ ROBUST
- ☐ HERBAL
- ☐ SKINKY
- ☐ CARAMEL
- ☐ MOLDY/BLUE
- ☐ NUTTY
- ☐ EARTHY

MILK
- ☐ COW
- ☐ SHEEP
- ☐ GOAT
- ☐ RAW
- ☐ OTHER: _____
  _____
  _____

TEXTURE METER
- RUNNY
- SOFT
- SEMI-SOFT
- SEMI-FIRM
- FIRM
- HARD

NOTES
_____
_____
_____
_____
_____
_____

RATING
☆☆☆☆☆

NAME OF CHEESE _____

FACTORY _____

RIND
- ☐ BLOOMY ☐ WASHED ☐ NATURAL ☐ DRY
  - ☐ WHITE   ☐ SALTY   ☐ THICK
  - ☐ SOFT   ☐ HARD
  - ☐ FUZZY   ☐ GRITTY

ORIGIN _____

DATE _____

PRICE _____

FLAVORS
- ☐ SALTY   ☐ GRASSY
- ☐ SWEET   ☐ ROBUST
- ☐ CRYSTALLINE   ☐ HERBAL
- ☐ CRUMBLY   ☐ SKINKY
- ☐ SHARP/TANGY   ☐ CARAMEL
- ☐ MILKY/LACTIC   ☐ MOLDY/BLUE
- ☐ LEMON   ☐ NUTTY
- ☐ BUTTERY/CREAMY   ☐ EARTHY

MILK
- ☐ COW
- ☐ SHEEP
- ☐ GOAT
- ☐ RAW
- ☐ OTHER: _____

TEXTURE METER
- RUNNY
- SOFT
- SEMI-SOFT
- SEMI-FIRM
- FIRM
- HARD

NOTES
_____
_____
_____
_____
_____
_____

RATING
☆ ☆ ☆ ☆ ☆

NAME OF CHEESE _____

FACTORY _____

RIND
- [ ] BLOOMY
- [ ] WASHED
- [ ] NATURAL
- [ ] DRY
  - [ ] WHITE
  - [ ] SALTY
  - [ ] THICK
  - [ ] SOFT
  - [ ] HARD
  - [ ] FUZZY
  - [ ] GRITTY

ORIGIN _____

DATE _____

PRICE _____

FLAVORS
- [ ] SALTY
- [ ] GRASSY
- [ ] SWEET
- [ ] ROBUST
- [ ] CRYSTALLINE
- [ ] HERBAL
- [ ] CRUMBLY
- [ ] SKINKY
- [ ] SHARP/TANGY
- [ ] CARAMEL
- [ ] MILKY/LACTIC
- [ ] MOLDY/BLUE
- [ ] LEMON
- [ ] NUTTY
- [ ] BUTTERY/CREAMY
- [ ] EARTHY

MILK
- [ ] COW
- [ ] SHEEP
- [ ] GOAT
- [ ] RAW
- [ ] OTHER: _____
  _____
  _____

TEXTURE METER
- RUNNY
- SOFT
- SEMI-SOFT
- SEMI-FIRM
- FIRM
- HARD

NOTES
_____
_____
_____
_____
_____
_____

RATING ☆☆☆☆☆

NAME OF CHEESE _____

FACTORY _____

RIND
☐ BLOOMY ☐ WASHED ☐ NATURAL ☐ DRY
☐ WHITE ☐ SALTY ☐ THICK
☐ SOFT ☐ HARD
☐ FUZZY ☐ GRITTY

ORIGIN _____

DATE _____

PRICE _____

FLAVORS		MILK	TEXTURE METER
☐ SALTY	☐ GRASSY	☐ COW	RUNNY
☐ SWEET	☐ ROBUST	☐ SHEEP	SOFT
☐ CRYSTALLINE	☐ HERBAL	☐ GOAT	SEMI-SOFT
☐ CRUMBLY	☐ SKINKY	☐ RAW	SEMI-FIRM
☐ SHARP/TANGY	☐ CARAMEL	☐ OTHER:	FIRM
☐ MILKY/LACTIC	☐ MOLDY/BLUE	_____	HARD
☐ LEMON	☐ NUTTY	_____	
☐ BUTTERY/CREAMY	☐ EARTHY	_____	

NOTES

_____

_____

_____

_____

_____

RATING
☆ ☆ ☆ ☆ ☆

NAME OF CHEESE _____

FACTORY _____

RIND

- [ ] BLOOMY   - [ ] WASHED   - [ ] NATURAL   - [ ] DRY
  - [ ] WHITE   - [ ] SALTY   - [ ] THICK
  - [ ] SOFT   - [ ] HARD
  - [ ] FUZZY   - [ ] GRITTY

ORIGIN _____

DATE _____

PRICE _____

FLAVORS

- [ ] SALTY
- [ ] SWEET
- [ ] CRYSTALLINE
- [ ] CRUMBLY
- [ ] SHARP/TANGY
- [ ] MILKY/LACTIC
- [ ] LEMON
- [ ] BUTTERY/CREAMY
- [ ] GRASSY
- [ ] ROBUST
- [ ] HERBAL
- [ ] SKINKY
- [ ] CARAMEL
- [ ] MOLDY/BLUE
- [ ] NUTTY
- [ ] EARTHY

MILK

- [ ] COW
- [ ] SHEEP
- [ ] GOAT
- [ ] RAW
- [ ] OTHER:
  _____
  _____
  _____

TEXTURE METER

- RUNNY
- SOFT
- SEMI-SOFT
- SEMI-FIRM
- FIRM
- HARD

NOTES

_____
_____
_____
_____
_____
_____

RATING
☆☆☆☆☆

NAME OF CHEESE _____

FACTORY _____

RIND
- ☐ BLOOMY ☐ WASHED ☐ NATURAL ☐ DRY
  - ☐ WHITE ☐ SALTY ☐ THICK
  - ☐ SOFT ☐ HARD
  - ☐ FUZZY ☐ GRITTY

ORIGIN _____

DATE _____

PRICE _____

FLAVORS
- ☐ SALTY
- ☐ SWEET
- ☐ CRYSTALLINE
- ☐ CRUMBLY
- ☐ SHARP/TANGY
- ☐ MILKY/LACTIC
- ☐ LEMON
- ☐ BUTTERY/CREAMY
- ☐ GRASSY
- ☐ ROBUST
- ☐ HERBAL
- ☐ SKINKY
- ☐ CARAMEL
- ☐ MOLDY/BLUE
- ☐ NUTTY
- ☐ EARTHY

MILK
- ☐ COW
- ☐ SHEEP
- ☐ GOAT
- ☐ RAW
- ☐ OTHER: _____

TEXTURE METER
- RUNNY
- SOFT
- SEMI-SOFT
- SEMI-FIRM
- FIRM
- HARD

NOTES
_____
_____
_____
_____
_____

RATING
☆☆☆☆☆

NAME OF CHEESE _____

FACTORY _____

RIND
- [ ] BLOOMY
- [ ] WASHED
- [ ] NATURAL
- [ ] DRY
  - [ ] WHITE
  - [ ] SOFT
  - [ ] FUZZY
  - [ ] SALTY
  - [ ] THICK
  - [ ] HARD
  - [ ] GRITTY

ORIGIN _____

DATE _____

PRICE _____

FLAVORS
- [ ] SALTY
- [ ] SWEET
- [ ] CRYSTALLINE
- [ ] CRUMBLY
- [ ] SHARP/TANGY
- [ ] MILKY/LACTIC
- [ ] LEMON
- [ ] BUTTERY/CREAMY
- [ ] GRASSY
- [ ] ROBUST
- [ ] HERBAL
- [ ] SKINKY
- [ ] CARAMEL
- [ ] MOLDY/BLUE
- [ ] NUTTY
- [ ] EARTHY

MILK
- [ ] COW
- [ ] SHEEP
- [ ] GOAT
- [ ] RAW
- [ ] OTHER: _____
  _____
  _____

TEXTURE METER
- RUNNY
- SOFT
- SEMI-SOFT
- SEMI-FIRM
- FIRM
- HARD

NOTES
_____
_____
_____
_____
_____
_____

RATING
☆☆☆☆☆

NAME OF CHEESE _____

FACTORY _____

RIND

- ☐ BLOOMY ☐ WASHED ☐ NATURAL ☐ DRY
  - ☐ WHITE   ☐ SALTY   ☐ THICK
  - ☐ SOFT   ☐ HARD
  - ☐ FUZZY   ☐ GRITTY

ORIGIN _____

DATE _____

PRICE _____

FLAVORS

- ☐ SALTY
- ☐ SWEET
- ☐ CRYSTALLINE
- ☐ CRUMBLY
- ☐ SHARP/TANGY
- ☐ MILKY/LACTIC
- ☐ LEMON
- ☐ BUTTERY/CREAMY
- ☐ GRASSY
- ☐ ROBUST
- ☐ HERBAL
- ☐ SKINKY
- ☐ CARAMEL
- ☐ MOLDY/BLUE
- ☐ NUTTY
- ☐ EARTHY

MILK

- ☐ COW
- ☐ SHEEP
- ☐ GOAT
- ☐ RAW
- ☐ OTHER: _____

TEXTURE METER

- RUNNY
- SOFT
- SEMI-SOFT
- SEMI-FIRM
- FIRM
- HARD

NOTES

_____
_____
_____
_____
_____

RATING

☆☆☆☆☆

NAME OF CHEESE _____

FACTORY _____

RIND

- ☐ BLOOMY ☐ WASHED ☐ NATURAL ☐ DRY
  - ☐ WHITE ☐ SALTY ☐ THICK
  - ☐ SOFT ☐ HARD
  - ☐ FUZZY ☐ GRITTY

ORIGIN _____

DATE _____

PRICE _____

FLAVORS

- ☐ SALTY ☐ GRASSY
- ☐ SWEET ☐ ROBUST
- ☐ CRYSTALLINE ☐ HERBAL
- ☐ CRUMBLY ☐ SKINKY
- ☐ SHARP/TANGY ☐ CARAMEL
- ☐ MILKY/LACTIC ☐ MOLDY/BLUE
- ☐ LEMON ☐ NUTTY
- ☐ BUTTERY/CREAMY ☐ EARTHY

MILK

- ☐ COW
- ☐ SHEEP
- ☐ GOAT
- ☐ RAW
- ☐ OTHER: _____
  _____
  _____

TEXTURE METER

- RUNNY
- SOFT
- SEMI-SOFT
- SEMI-FIRM
- FIRM
- HARD

NOTES

_____
_____
_____
_____
_____
_____

RATING ☆☆☆☆☆

NAME OF CHEESE _____

FACTORY _____

RIND
- ☐ BLOOMY ☐ WASHED ☐ NATURAL ☐ DRY
  - ☐ WHITE ☐ SALTY ☐ THICK
  - ☐ SOFT ☐ HARD
  - ☐ FUZZY ☐ GRITTY

ORIGIN _____

DATE _____

PRICE _____

FLAVORS
- ☐ SALTY
- ☐ SWEET
- ☐ CRYSTALLINE
- ☐ CRUMBLY
- ☐ SHARP/TANGY
- ☐ MILKY/LACTIC
- ☐ LEMON
- ☐ BUTTERY/CREAMY
- ☐ GRASSY
- ☐ ROBUST
- ☐ HERBAL
- ☐ SKINKY
- ☐ CARAMEL
- ☐ MOLDY/BLUE
- ☐ NUTTY
- ☐ EARTHY

MILK
- ☐ COW
- ☐ SHEEP
- ☐ GOAT
- ☐ RAW
- ☐ OTHER: _____
  _____
  _____

TEXTURE METER
- RUNNY
- SOFT
- SEMI-SOFT
- SEMI-FIRM
- FIRM
- HARD

NOTES
_____
_____
_____
_____
_____
_____

RATING ☆☆☆☆☆

NAME OF CHEESE _____

FACTORY _____

RIND
- ☐ BLOOMY ☐ WASHED ☐ NATURAL ☐ DRY
  - ☐ WHITE ☐ SALTY ☐ THICK
  - ☐ SOFT ☐ HARD
  - ☐ FUZZY ☐ GRITTY

ORIGIN _____

DATE _____

PRICE _____

FLAVORS
- ☐ SALTY
- ☐ SWEET
- ☐ CRYSTALLINE
- ☐ CRUMBLY
- ☐ SHARP/TANGY
- ☐ MILKY/LACTIC
- ☐ LEMON
- ☐ BUTTERY/CREAMY
- ☐ GRASSY
- ☐ ROBUST
- ☐ HERBAL
- ☐ SKINKY
- ☐ CARAMEL
- ☐ MOLDY/BLUE
- ☐ NUTTY
- ☐ EARTHY

MILK
- ☐ COW
- ☐ SHEEP
- ☐ GOAT
- ☐ RAW
- ☐ OTHER: _____
  _____
  _____

TEXTURE METER
- RUNNY
- SOFT
- SEMI-SOFT
- SEMI-FIRM
- FIRM
- HARD

NOTES
_____
_____
_____
_____
_____
_____

RATING
☆☆☆☆☆

NAME OF CHEESE _____

FACTORY _____

RIND
- ☐ BLOOMY ☐ WASHED ☐ NATURAL ☐ DRY
  - ☐ WHITE   ☐ SALTY   ☐ THICK
  - ☐ SOFT   ☐ HARD
  - ☐ FUZZY   ☐ GRITTY

ORIGIN _____

DATE _____

PRICE _____

FLAVORS
- ☐ SALTY
- ☐ SWEET
- ☐ CRYSTALLINE
- ☐ CRUMBLY
- ☐ SHARP/TANGY
- ☐ MILKY/LACTIC
- ☐ LEMON
- ☐ BUTTERY/CREAMY
- ☐ GRASSY
- ☐ ROBUST
- ☐ HERBAL
- ☐ SKINKY
- ☐ CARAMEL
- ☐ MOLDY/BLUE
- ☐ NUTTY
- ☐ EARTHY

MILK
- ☐ COW
- ☐ SHEEP
- ☐ GOAT
- ☐ RAW
- ☐ OTHER: _____
  _____
  _____

TEXTURE METER
- RUNNY
- SOFT
- SEMI-SOFT
- SEMI-FIRM
- FIRM
- HARD

NOTES
_____
_____
_____
_____
_____
_____

RATING
☆ ☆ ☆ ☆ ☆

NAME OF CHEESE _____

FACTORY _____

RIND
- [ ] BLOOMY
- [ ] WASHED
- [ ] NATURAL
- [ ] DRY
  - [ ] WHITE
  - [ ] SOFT
  - [ ] FUZZY
  - [ ] SALTY
  - [ ] THICK
  - [ ] HARD
  - [ ] GRITTY

ORIGIN _____

DATE _____

PRICE _____

FLAVORS
- [ ] SALTY
- [ ] SWEET
- [ ] CRYSTALLINE
- [ ] CRUMBLY
- [ ] SHARP/TANGY
- [ ] MILKY/LACTIC
- [ ] LEMON
- [ ] BUTTERY/CREAMY
- [ ] GRASSY
- [ ] ROBUST
- [ ] HERBAL
- [ ] SKINKY
- [ ] CARAMEL
- [ ] MOLDY/BLUE
- [ ] NUTTY
- [ ] EARTHY

MILK
- [ ] COW
- [ ] SHEEP
- [ ] GOAT
- [ ] RAW
- [ ] OTHER: _____
  _____
  _____

TEXTURE METER
- RUNNY
- SOFT
- SEMI-SOFT
- SEMI-FIRM
- FIRM
- HARD

NOTES
_____
_____
_____
_____
_____
_____

RATING
☆ ☆ ☆ ☆ ☆

NAME OF CHEESE _____

FACTORY _____

RIND

- [ ] BLOOMY
- [ ] WASHED
- [ ] NATURAL
- [ ] DRY
  - [ ] WHITE
  - [ ] SALTY
  - [ ] THICK
  - [ ] SOFT
  - [ ] HARD
  - [ ] FUZZY
  - [ ] GRITTY

ORIGIN _____

DATE _____

PRICE _____

FLAVORS

- [ ] SALTY
- [ ] GRASSY
- [ ] SWEET
- [ ] ROBUST
- [ ] CRYSTALLINE
- [ ] HERBAL
- [ ] CRUMBLY
- [ ] SKINKY
- [ ] SHARP/TANGY
- [ ] CARAMEL
- [ ] MILKY/LACTIC
- [ ] MOLDY/BLUE
- [ ] LEMON
- [ ] NUTTY
- [ ] BUTTERY/CREAMY
- [ ] EARTHY

MILK

- [ ] COW
- [ ] SHEEP
- [ ] GOAT
- [ ] RAW
- [ ] OTHER: _____
  _____
  _____

TEXTURE METER

- RUNNY
- SOFT
- SEMI-SOFT
- SEMI-FIRM
- FIRM
- HARD

NOTES

_____
_____
_____
_____
_____

RATING

☆ ☆ ☆ ☆ ☆

NAME OF CHEESE _____

FACTORY _____

RIND
- ☐ BLOOMY ☐ WASHED ☐ NATURAL ☐ DRY
  - ☐ WHITE   ☐ SALTY   ☐ THICK
  - ☐ SOFT   ☐ HARD
  - ☐ FUZZY   ☐ GRITTY

ORIGIN _____

DATE _____

PRICE _____

FLAVORS
- ☐ SALTY
- ☐ SWEET
- ☐ CRYSTALLINE
- ☐ CRUMBLY
- ☐ SHARP/TANGY
- ☐ MILKY/LACTIC
- ☐ LEMON
- ☐ BUTTERY/CREAMY
- ☐ GRASSY
- ☐ ROBUST
- ☐ HERBAL
- ☐ SKINKY
- ☐ CARAMEL
- ☐ MOLDY/BLUE
- ☐ NUTTY
- ☐ EARTHY

MILK
- ☐ COW
- ☐ SHEEP
- ☐ GOAT
- ☐ RAW
- ☐ OTHER: _____ _____ _____

TEXTURE METER
- RUNNY
- SOFT
- SEMI-SOFT
- SEMI-FIRM
- FIRM
- HARD

NOTES
_____
_____
_____
_____
_____
_____

RATING ☆☆☆☆☆

NAME OF CHEESE _____

FACTORY _____

RIND

- ☐ BLOOMY ☐ WASHED ☐ NATURAL ☐ DRY
  - ☐ WHITE   ☐ SALTY   ☐ THICK
  - ☐ SOFT   ☐ HARD
  - ☐ FUZZY   ☐ GRITTY

ORIGIN _____

DATE _____

PRICE _____

FLAVORS

- ☐ SALTY
- ☐ SWEET
- ☐ CRYSTALLINE
- ☐ CRUMBLY
- ☐ SHARP/TANGY
- ☐ MILKY/LACTIC
- ☐ LEMON
- ☐ BUTTERY/CREAMY
- ☐ GRASSY
- ☐ ROBUST
- ☐ HERBAL
- ☐ SKINKY
- ☐ CARAMEL
- ☐ MOLDY/BLUE
- ☐ NUTTY
- ☐ EARTHY

MILK

- ☐ COW
- ☐ SHEEP
- ☐ GOAT
- ☐ RAW
- ☐ OTHER: _____
  _____
  _____

TEXTURE METER

- RUNNY
- SOFT
- SEMI-SOFT
- SEMI-FIRM
- FIRM
- HARD

NOTES

_____
_____
_____
_____
_____
_____

RATING

☆☆☆☆☆

NAME OF CHEESE _____

FACTORY _____

RIND

- [ ] BLOOMY
- [ ] WASHED
- [ ] NATURAL
- [ ] DRY
  - [ ] WHITE
  - [ ] SALTY
  - [ ] THICK
  - [ ] SOFT
  - [ ] HARD
  - [ ] FUZZY
  - [ ] GRITTY

ORIGIN _____

DATE _____

PRICE _____

FLAVORS

- [ ] SALTY
- [ ] SWEET
- [ ] CRYSTALLINE
- [ ] CRUMBLY
- [ ] SHARP/TANGY
- [ ] MILKY/LACTIC
- [ ] LEMON
- [ ] BUTTERY/CREAMY
- [ ] GRASSY
- [ ] ROBUST
- [ ] HERBAL
- [ ] SKINKY
- [ ] CARAMEL
- [ ] MOLDY/BLUE
- [ ] NUTTY
- [ ] EARTHY

MILK

- [ ] COW
- [ ] SHEEP
- [ ] GOAT
- [ ] RAW
- [ ] OTHER: _____
  _____
  _____

TEXTURE METER

- RUNNY
- SOFT
- SEMI-SOFT
- SEMI-FIRM
- FIRM
- HARD

NOTES

_____
_____
_____
_____
_____
_____
_____

RATING

☆ ☆ ☆ ☆ ☆

NAME OF CHEESE _____

FACTORY _____

RIND
- ☐ BLOOMY ☐ WASHED ☐ NATURAL ☐ DRY
  - ☐ WHITE ☐ SALTY ☐ THICK
  - ☐ SOFT ☐ HARD
  - ☐ FUZZY ☐ GRITTY

ORIGIN _____

DATE _____

PRICE _____

FLAVORS
- ☐ SALTY ☐ GRASSY
- ☐ SWEET ☐ ROBUST
- ☐ CRYSTALLINE ☐ HERBAL
- ☐ CRUMBLY ☐ SKINKY
- ☐ SHARP/TANGY ☐ CARAMEL
- ☐ MILKY/LACTIC ☐ MOLDY/BLUE
- ☐ LEMON ☐ NUTTY
- ☐ BUTTERY/CREAMY ☐ EARTHY

MILK
- ☐ COW
- ☐ SHEEP
- ☐ GOAT
- ☐ RAW
- ☐ OTHER: _____
  _____
  _____

TEXTURE METER
- RUNNY
- SOFT
- SEMI-SOFT
- SEMI-FIRM
- FIRM
- HARD

NOTES
_____
_____
_____
_____
_____

RATING ☆☆☆☆☆

NAME OF CHEESE _____

FACTORY _____

RIND
- ☐ BLOOMY ☐ WASHED ☐ NATURAL ☐ DRY
  - ☐ WHITE ☐ SALTY ☐ THICK
  - ☐ SOFT ☐ HARD
  - ☐ FUZZY ☐ GRITTY

ORIGIN _____

DATE _____

PRICE _____

FLAVORS
- ☐ SALTY
- ☐ SWEET
- ☐ CRYSTALLINE
- ☐ CRUMBLY
- ☐ SHARP/TANGY
- ☐ MILKY/LACTIC
- ☐ LEMON
- ☐ BUTTERY/CREAMY
- ☐ GRASSY
- ☐ ROBUST
- ☐ HERBAL
- ☐ SKINKY
- ☐ CARAMEL
- ☐ MOLDY/BLUE
- ☐ NUTTY
- ☐ EARTHY

MILK
- ☐ COW
- ☐ SHEEP
- ☐ GOAT
- ☐ RAW
- ☐ OTHER: _____
  _____
  _____

TEXTURE METER
- RUNNY
- SOFT
- SEMI-SOFT
- SEMI-FIRM
- FIRM
- HARD

NOTES
_____
_____
_____
_____
_____
_____

RATING ☆☆☆☆☆

NAME OF CHEESE _____

FACTORY _____

RIND
- ☐ BLOOMY   ☐ WASHED   ☐ NATURAL   ☐ DRY
  - ☐ WHITE   ☐ SALTY   ☐ THICK
  - ☐ SOFT   ☐ HARD
  - ☐ FUZZY   ☐ GRITTY

ORIGIN _____

DATE _____

PRICE _____

FLAVORS
- ☐ SALTY
- ☐ SWEET
- ☐ CRYSTALLINE
- ☐ CRUMBLY
- ☐ SHARP/TANGY
- ☐ MILKY/LACTIC
- ☐ LEMON
- ☐ BUTTERY/CREAMY
- ☐ GRASSY
- ☐ ROBUST
- ☐ HERBAL
- ☐ SKINKY
- ☐ CARAMEL
- ☐ MOLDY/BLUE
- ☐ NUTTY
- ☐ EARTHY

MILK
- ☐ COW
- ☐ SHEEP
- ☐ GOAT
- ☐ RAW
- ☐ OTHER: _____
  _____
  _____

TEXTURE METER
- RUNNY
- SOFT
- SEMI-SOFT
- SEMI-FIRM
- FIRM
- HARD

NOTES
_____
_____
_____
_____
_____
_____

RATING
☆ ☆ ☆ ☆ ☆

NAME OF CHEESE _____

FACTORY _____

RIND

- [ ] BLOOMY
- [ ] WASHED
- [ ] NATURAL
- [ ] DRY
  - [ ] WHITE
  - [ ] SALTY
  - [ ] THICK
  - [ ] SOFT
  - [ ] HARD
  - [ ] FUZZY
  - [ ] GRITTY

ORIGIN _____

DATE _____

PRICE _____

FLAVORS

- [ ] SALTY
- [ ] GRASSY
- [ ] SWEET
- [ ] ROBUST
- [ ] CRYSTALLINE
- [ ] HERBAL
- [ ] CRUMBLY
- [ ] SKINKY
- [ ] SHARP/TANGY
- [ ] CARAMEL
- [ ] MILKY/LACTIC
- [ ] MOLDY/BLUE
- [ ] LEMON
- [ ] NUTTY
- [ ] BUTTERY/CREAMY
- [ ] EARTHY

MILK

- [ ] COW
- [ ] SHEEP
- [ ] GOAT
- [ ] RAW
- [ ] OTHER: _____
  _____
  _____

TEXTURE METER

- RUNNY
- SOFT
- SEMI-SOFT
- SEMI-FIRM
- FIRM
- HARD

NOTES

_____
_____
_____
_____
_____
_____

RATING

☆ ☆ ☆ ☆ ☆

NAME OF CHEESE _____

FACTORY _____

RIND
- ☐ BLOOMY ☐ WASHED ☐ NATURAL ☐ DRY
  - ☐ WHITE ☐ SALTY ☐ THICK
  - ☐ SOFT ☐ HARD
  - ☐ FUZZY ☐ GRITTY

ORIGIN _____

DATE _____

PRICE _____

FLAVORS
- ☐ SALTY ☐ GRASSY
- ☐ SWEET ☐ ROBUST
- ☐ CRYSTALLINE ☐ HERBAL
- ☐ CRUMBLY ☐ SKINKY
- ☐ SHARP/TANGY ☐ CARAMEL
- ☐ MILKY/LACTIC ☐ MOLDY/BLUE
- ☐ LEMON ☐ NUTTY
- ☐ BUTTERY/CREAMY ☐ EARTHY

MILK
- ☐ COW
- ☐ SHEEP
- ☐ GOAT
- ☐ RAW
- ☐ OTHER: _____
  _____
  _____

TEXTURE METER
- RUNNY
- SOFT
- SEMI-SOFT
- SEMI-FIRM
- FIRM
- HARD

NOTES
_____
_____
_____
_____
_____
_____

RATING ☆☆☆☆☆

NAME OF CHEESE _____

FACTORY _____

RIND
- ☐ BLOOMY   ☐ WASHED   ☐ NATURAL   ☐ DRY
  - ☐ WHITE   ☐ SALTY   ☐ THICK
  - ☐ SOFT   ☐ HARD
  - ☐ FUZZY   ☐ GRITTY

ORIGIN _____

DATE _____

PRICE _____

FLAVORS
- ☐ SALTY
- ☐ SWEET
- ☐ CRYSTALLINE
- ☐ CRUMBLY
- ☐ SHARP/TANGY
- ☐ MILKY/LACTIC
- ☐ LEMON
- ☐ BUTTERY/CREAMY
- ☐ GRASSY
- ☐ ROBUST
- ☐ HERBAL
- ☐ SKINKY
- ☐ CARAMEL
- ☐ MOLDY/BLUE
- ☐ NUTTY
- ☐ EARTHY

MILK
- ☐ COW
- ☐ SHEEP
- ☐ GOAT
- ☐ RAW
- ☐ OTHER: _____

TEXTURE METER
- RUNNY
- SOFT
- SEMI-SOFT
- SEMI-FIRM
- FIRM
- HARD

NOTES
_____
_____
_____
_____
_____
_____

RATING ☆☆☆☆☆

NAME OF CHEESE _____

FACTORY _____

RIND
- ☐ BLOOMY ☐ WASHED ☐ NATURAL ☐ DRY
  - ☐ WHITE   ☐ SALTY   ☐ THICK
  - ☐ SOFT   ☐ HARD
  - ☐ FUZZY   ☐ GRITTY

ORIGIN _____

DATE _____

PRICE _____

FLAVORS
- ☐ SALTY   ☐ GRASSY
- ☐ SWEET   ☐ ROBUST
- ☐ CRYSTALLINE   ☐ HERBAL
- ☐ CRUMBLY   ☐ SKINKY
- ☐ SHARP/TANGY   ☐ CARAMEL
- ☐ MILKY/LACTIC   ☐ MOLDY/BLUE
- ☐ LEMON   ☐ NUTTY
- ☐ BUTTERY/CREAMY   ☐ EARTHY

MILK
- ☐ COW
- ☐ SHEEP
- ☐ GOAT
- ☐ RAW
- ☐ OTHER: _____
  _____
  _____

TEXTURE METER
- RUNNY
- SOFT
- SEMI-SOFT
- SEMI-FIRM
- FIRM
- HARD

NOTES
_____
_____
_____
_____
_____
_____

RATING
☆ ☆ ☆ ☆ ☆

NAME OF CHEESE _____

FACTORY _____

RIND
- ☐ BLOOMY   ☐ WASHED   ☐ NATURAL   ☐ DRY
  - ☐ WHITE   ☐ SALTY   ☐ THICK
  - ☐ SOFT   ☐ HARD
  - ☐ FUZZY   ☐ GRITTY

ORIGIN _____

DATE _____

PRICE _____

FLAVORS
- ☐ SALTY   ☐ GRASSY
- ☐ SWEET   ☐ ROBUST
- ☐ CRYSTALLINE ☐ HERBAL
- ☐ CRUMBLY   ☐ SKINKY
- ☐ SHARP/TANGY ☐ CARAMEL
- ☐ MILKY/LACTIC ☐ MOLDY/BLUE
- ☐ LEMON   ☐ NUTTY
- ☐ BUTTERY/CREAMY ☐ EARTHY

MILK
- ☐ COW
- ☐ SHEEP
- ☐ GOAT
- ☐ RAW
- ☐ OTHER: _____
  _____
  _____

TEXTURE METER
- RUNNY
- SOFT
- SEMI-SOFT
- SEMI-FIRM
- FIRM
- HARD

NOTES
_____
_____
_____
_____
_____
_____

RATING ☆☆☆☆☆

NAME OF CHEESE _____

FACTORY _____

RIND
- ☐ BLOOMY ☐ WASHED ☐ NATURAL ☐ DRY
  - ☐ WHITE ☐ SALTY ☐ THICK
  - ☐ SOFT   ☐ HARD
  - ☐ FUZZY ☐ GRITTY

ORIGIN _____

DATE _____

PRICE _____

FLAVORS
- ☐ SALTY
- ☐ SWEET
- ☐ CRYSTALLINE
- ☐ CRUMBLY
- ☐ SHARP/TANGY
- ☐ MILKY/LACTIC
- ☐ LEMON
- ☐ BUTTERY/CREAMY
- ☐ GRASSY
- ☐ ROBUST
- ☐ HERBAL
- ☐ SKINKY
- ☐ CARAMEL
- ☐ MOLDY/BLUE
- ☐ NUTTY
- ☐ EARTHY

MILK
- ☐ COW
- ☐ SHEEP
- ☐ GOAT
- ☐ RAW
- ☐ OTHER: _____ _____ _____

TEXTURE METER
- RUNNY
- SOFT
- SEMI-SOFT
- SEMI-FIRM
- FIRM
- HARD

NOTES
_____
_____
_____
_____
_____

RATING ☆☆☆☆☆

NAME OF CHEESE _____

FACTORY _____

RIND
- [ ] BLOOMY
- [ ] WASHED
- [ ] NATURAL
- [ ] DRY
  - [ ] WHITE
  - [ ] SALTY
  - [ ] THICK
  - [ ] SOFT
  - [ ] HARD
  - [ ] FUZZY
  - [ ] GRITTY

ORIGIN _____

DATE _____

PRICE _____

FLAVORS
- [ ] SALTY
- [ ] GRASSY
- [ ] SWEET
- [ ] ROBUST
- [ ] CRYSTALLINE
- [ ] HERBAL
- [ ] CRUMBLY
- [ ] SKINKY
- [ ] SHARP/TANGY
- [ ] CARAMEL
- [ ] MILKY/LACTIC
- [ ] MOLDY/BLUE
- [ ] LEMON
- [ ] NUTTY
- [ ] BUTTERY/CREAMY
- [ ] EARTHY

MILK
- [ ] COW
- [ ] SHEEP
- [ ] GOAT
- [ ] RAW
- [ ] OTHER: _____
_____
_____

TEXTURE METER
- RUNNY
- SOFT
- SEMI-SOFT
- SEMI-FIRM
- FIRM
- HARD

NOTES
_____
_____
_____
_____
_____
_____

RATING
☆ ☆ ☆ ☆ ☆

NAME OF CHEESE _____

FACTORY _____

RIND

- ☐ BLOOMY   ☐ WASHED   ☐ NATURAL   ☐ DRY
  - ☐ WHITE   ☐ SALTY   ☐ THICK
  - ☐ SOFT   ☐ HARD
  - ☐ FUZZY   ☐ GRITTY

ORIGIN _____

DATE _____

PRICE _____

FLAVORS

- ☐ SALTY
- ☐ SWEET
- ☐ CRYSTALLINE
- ☐ CRUMBLY
- ☐ SHARP/TANGY
- ☐ MILKY/LACTIC
- ☐ LEMON
- ☐ BUTTERY/CREAMY
- ☐ GRASSY
- ☐ ROBUST
- ☐ HERBAL
- ☐ SKINKY
- ☐ CARAMEL
- ☐ MOLDY/BLUE
- ☐ NUTTY
- ☐ EARTHY

MILK

- ☐ COW
- ☐ SHEEP
- ☐ GOAT
- ☐ RAW
- ☐ OTHER: _____
  _____
  _____

TEXTURE METER

- RUNNY
- SOFT
- SEMI-SOFT
- SEMI-FIRM
- FIRM
- HARD

NOTES

_____
_____
_____
_____
_____
_____

RATING

☆ ☆ ☆ ☆ ☆

NAME OF CHEESE _____

FACTORY _____

RIND
- [ ] BLOOMY
- [ ] WASHED
- [ ] NATURAL
- [ ] DRY
  - [ ] WHITE
  - [ ] SALTY
  - [ ] THICK
  - [ ] SOFT
  - [ ] HARD
  - [ ] FUZZY
  - [ ] GRITTY

ORIGIN _____

DATE _____

PRICE _____

FLAVORS
- [ ] SALTY
- [ ] GRASSY
- [ ] SWEET
- [ ] ROBUST
- [ ] CRYSTALLINE
- [ ] HERBAL
- [ ] CRUMBLY
- [ ] SKINKY
- [ ] SHARP/TANGY
- [ ] CARAMEL
- [ ] MILKY/LACTIC
- [ ] MOLDY/BLUE
- [ ] LEMON
- [ ] NUTTY
- [ ] BUTTERY/CREAMY
- [ ] EARTHY

MILK
- [ ] COW
- [ ] SHEEP
- [ ] GOAT
- [ ] RAW
- [ ] OTHER: _____

TEXTURE METER
- RUNNY
- SOFT
- SEMI-SOFT
- SEMI-FIRM
- FIRM
- HARD

NOTES
_____
_____
_____
_____
_____
_____

RATING
☆☆☆☆☆

NAME OF CHEESE _____

FACTORY _____

RIND
- ☐ BLOOMY ☐ WASHED ☐ NATURAL ☐ DRY
  - ☐ WHITE   ☐ SALTY   ☐ THICK
  - ☐ SOFT   ☐ HARD
  - ☐ FUZZY   ☐ GRITTY

ORIGIN _____

DATE _____

PRICE _____

FLAVORS
- ☐ SALTY   ☐ GRASSY
- ☐ SWEET   ☐ ROBUST
- ☐ CRYSTALLINE   ☐ HERBAL
- ☐ CRUMBLY   ☐ SKINKY
- ☐ SHARP/TANGY   ☐ CARAMEL
- ☐ MILKY/LACTIC   ☐ MOLDY/BLUE
- ☐ LEMON   ☐ NUTTY
- ☐ BUTTERY/CREAMY   ☐ EARTHY

MILK
- ☐ COW
- ☐ SHEEP
- ☐ GOAT
- ☐ RAW
- ☐ OTHER: _____

TEXTURE METER
- RUNNY
- SOFT
- SEMI-SOFT
- SEMI-FIRM
- FIRM
- HARD

NOTES
_____
_____
_____
_____
_____
_____

RATING ☆☆☆☆☆

NAME OF CHEESE _____

FACTORY _____

RIND
- [ ] BLOOMY
- [ ] WASHED
- [ ] NATURAL
- [ ] DRY
  - [ ] WHITE
  - [ ] SALTY
  - [ ] THICK
  - [ ] SOFT
  - [ ] HARD
  - [ ] FUZZY
  - [ ] GRITTY

ORIGIN _____

DATE _____

PRICE _____

FLAVORS
- [ ] SALTY
- [ ] GRASSY
- [ ] SWEET
- [ ] ROBUST
- [ ] CRYSTALLINE
- [ ] HERBAL
- [ ] CRUMBLY
- [ ] SKINKY
- [ ] SHARP/TANGY
- [ ] CARAMEL
- [ ] MILKY/LACTIC
- [ ] MOLDY/BLUE
- [ ] LEMON
- [ ] NUTTY
- [ ] BUTTERY/CREAMY
- [ ] EARTHY

MILK
- [ ] COW
- [ ] SHEEP
- [ ] GOAT
- [ ] RAW
- [ ] OTHER: _____
  _____
  _____

TEXTURE METER
- RUNNY
- SOFT
- SEMI-SOFT
- SEMI-FIRM
- FIRM
- HARD

NOTES
_____
_____
_____
_____
_____

RATING
☆☆☆☆☆

NAME OF CHEESE _____

FACTORY _____

RIND
- ☐ BLOOMY ☐ WASHED ☐ NATURAL ☐ DRY
  - ☐ WHITE ☐ SALTY ☐ THICK
  - ☐ SOFT   ☐ HARD
  - ☐ FUZZY ☐ GRITTY

ORIGIN _____

DATE _____

PRICE _____

FLAVORS
- ☐ SALTY
- ☐ SWEET
- ☐ CRYSTALLINE
- ☐ CRUMBLY
- ☐ SHARP/TANGY
- ☐ MILKY/LACTIC
- ☐ LEMON
- ☐ BUTTERY/CREAMY
- ☐ GRASSY
- ☐ ROBUST
- ☐ HERBAL
- ☐ SKINKY
- ☐ CARAMEL
- ☐ MOLDY/BLUE
- ☐ NUTTY
- ☐ EARTHY

MILK
- ☐ COW
- ☐ SHEEP
- ☐ GOAT
- ☐ RAW
- ☐ OTHER: _____

TEXTURE METER
- RUNNY
- SOFT
- SEMI-SOFT
- SEMI-FIRM
- FIRM
- HARD

NOTES
_____
_____
_____
_____
_____
_____

RATING ☆☆☆☆☆

NAME OF CHEESE _____

FACTORY _____

RIND

- [ ] BLOOMY
- [ ] WASHED
- [ ] NATURAL
- [ ] DRY
  - [ ] WHITE
  - [ ] SALTY
  - [ ] THICK
  - [ ] SOFT
  - [ ] HARD
  - [ ] FUZZY
  - [ ] GRITTY

ORIGIN _____

DATE _____

PRICE _____

FLAVORS

- [ ] SALTY
- [ ] GRASSY
- [ ] SWEET
- [ ] ROBUST
- [ ] CRYSTALLINE
- [ ] HERBAL
- [ ] CRUMBLY
- [ ] SKINKY
- [ ] SHARP/TANGY
- [ ] CARAMEL
- [ ] MILKY/LACTIC
- [ ] MOLDY/BLUE
- [ ] LEMON
- [ ] NUTTY
- [ ] BUTTERY/CREAMY
- [ ] EARTHY

MILK

- [ ] COW
- [ ] SHEEP
- [ ] GOAT
- [ ] RAW
- [ ] OTHER: _____
  _____
  _____

TEXTURE METER

- RUNNY
- SOFT
- SEMI-SOFT
- SEMI-FIRM
- FIRM
- HARD

NOTES

_____
_____
_____
_____
_____
_____

RATING

☆☆☆☆☆

NAME OF CHEESE _____

FACTORY _____

RIND
- [ ] BLOOMY [ ] WASHED [ ] NATURAL [ ] DRY
  - [ ] WHITE [ ] SALTY [ ] THICK
  - [ ] SOFT   [ ] HARD
  - [ ] FUZZY   [ ] GRITTY

ORIGIN _____

DATE _____

PRICE _____

FLAVORS
- [ ] SALTY
- [ ] SWEET
- [ ] CRYSTALLINE
- [ ] CRUMBLY
- [ ] SHARP/TANGY
- [ ] MILKY/LACTIC
- [ ] LEMON
- [ ] BUTTERY/CREAMY
- [ ] GRASSY
- [ ] ROBUST
- [ ] HERBAL
- [ ] SKINKY
- [ ] CARAMEL
- [ ] MOLDY/BLUE
- [ ] NUTTY
- [ ] EARTHY

MILK
- [ ] COW
- [ ] SHEEP
- [ ] GOAT
- [ ] RAW
- [ ] OTHER: _____
  _____
  _____

TEXTURE METER
- RUNNY
- SOFT
- SEMI-SOFT
- SEMI-FIRM
- FIRM
- HARD

NOTES
_____
_____
_____
_____
_____

RATING
☆ ☆ ☆ ☆ ☆

NAME OF CHEESE _____

FACTORY _____

RIND
- ☐ BLOOMY ☐ WASHED ☐ NATURAL ☐ DRY
  - ☐ WHITE ☐ SALTY ☐ THICK
  - ☐ SOFT ☐ HARD
  - ☐ FUZZY ☐ GRITTY

ORIGIN _____

DATE _____

PRICE _____

FLAVORS
- ☐ SALTY ☐ GRASSY
- ☐ SWEET ☐ ROBUST
- ☐ CRYSTALLINE ☐ HERBAL
- ☐ CRUMBLY ☐ SKINKY
- ☐ SHARP/TANGY ☐ CARAMEL
- ☐ MILKY/LACTIC ☐ MOLDY/BLUE
- ☐ LEMON ☐ NUTTY
- ☐ BUTTERY/CREAMY ☐ EARTHY

MILK
- ☐ COW
- ☐ SHEEP
- ☐ GOAT
- ☐ RAW
- ☐ OTHER: _____
  _____
  _____

TEXTURE METER
- RUNNY
- SOFT
- SEMI-SOFT
- SEMI-FIRM
- FIRM
- HARD

NOTES
_____
_____
_____
_____
_____
_____

RATING ☆☆☆☆☆

NAME OF CHEESE _____

FACTORY _____

RIND

- ☐ BLOOMY   ☐ WASHED   ☐ NATURAL   ☐ DRY
  - ☐ WHITE   ☐ SALTY   ☐ THICK
  - ☐ SOFT   ☐ HARD
  - ☐ FUZZY   ☐ GRITTY

ORIGIN _____

DATE _____

PRICE _____

FLAVORS

- ☐ SALTY   ☐ GRASSY
- ☐ SWEET   ☐ ROBUST
- ☐ CRYSTALLINE   ☐ HERBAL
- ☐ CRUMBLY   ☐ SKINKY
- ☐ SHARP/TANGY   ☐ CARAMEL
- ☐ MILKY/LACTIC   ☐ MOLDY/BLUE
- ☐ LEMON   ☐ NUTTY
- ☐ BUTTERY/CREAMY   ☐ EARTHY

MILK

- ☐ COW
- ☐ SHEEP
- ☐ GOAT
- ☐ RAW
- ☐ OTHER:
  _____
  _____
  _____

TEXTURE METER

- RUNNY
- SOFT
- SEMI-SOFT
- SEMI-FIRM
- FIRM
- HARD

NOTES

_____
_____
_____
_____
_____
_____

RATING

☆ ☆ ☆ ☆ ☆

NAME OF CHEESE _____

FACTORY _____

RIND
- [ ] BLOOMY
- [ ] WASHED
- [ ] NATURAL
- [ ] DRY
    - [ ] WHITE
    - [ ] SOFT
    - [ ] FUZZY
    - [ ] SALTY
    - [ ] THICK
    - [ ] HARD
    - [ ] GRITTY

ORIGIN _____

DATE _____

PRICE _____

FLAVORS
- [ ] SALTY
- [ ] SWEET
- [ ] CRYSTALLINE
- [ ] CRUMBLY
- [ ] SHARP/TANGY
- [ ] MILKY/LACTIC
- [ ] LEMON
- [ ] BUTTERY/CREAMY
- [ ] GRASSY
- [ ] ROBUST
- [ ] HERBAL
- [ ] SKINKY
- [ ] CARAMEL
- [ ] MOLDY/BLUE
- [ ] NUTTY
- [ ] EARTHY

MILK
- [ ] COW
- [ ] SHEEP
- [ ] GOAT
- [ ] RAW
- [ ] OTHER: _____

TEXTURE METER
- RUNNY
- SOFT
- SEMI-SOFT
- SEMI-FIRM
- FIRM
- HARD

NOTES
_____
_____
_____
_____
_____
_____

RATING ☆☆☆☆☆

NAME OF CHEESE _____

FACTORY _____

RIND
- ☐ BLOOMY ☐ WASHED ☐ NATURAL ☐ DRY
  - ☐ WHITE ☐ SALTY ☐ THICK
  - ☐ SOFT ☐ HARD
  - ☐ FUZZY ☐ GRITTY

ORIGIN _____

DATE _____

PRICE _____

FLAVORS
- ☐ SALTY
- ☐ SWEET
- ☐ CRYSTALLINE
- ☐ CRUMBLY
- ☐ SHARP/TANGY
- ☐ MILKY/LACTIC
- ☐ LEMON
- ☐ BUTTERY/CREAMY
- ☐ GRASSY
- ☐ ROBUST
- ☐ HERBAL
- ☐ SKINKY
- ☐ CARAMEL
- ☐ MOLDY/BLUE
- ☐ NUTTY
- ☐ EARTHY

MILK
- ☐ COW
- ☐ SHEEP
- ☐ GOAT
- ☐ RAW
- ☐ OTHER: _____
  _____
  _____

TEXTURE METER
- RUNNY
- SOFT
- SEMI-SOFT
- SEMI-FIRM
- FIRM
- HARD

NOTES
_____
_____
_____
_____
_____

RATING
☆ ☆ ☆ ☆ ☆

NAME OF CHEESE _____

FACTORY _____

RIND
- [ ] BLOOMY
- [ ] WASHED
- [ ] NATURAL
- [ ] DRY
  - [ ] WHITE
  - [ ] SALTY
  - [ ] THICK
  - [ ] SOFT
  - [ ] HARD
  - [ ] FUZZY
  - [ ] GRITTY

ORIGIN _____

DATE _____

PRICE _____

FLAVORS
- [ ] SALTY
- [ ] GRASSY
- [ ] SWEET
- [ ] ROBUST
- [ ] CRYSTALLINE
- [ ] HERBAL
- [ ] CRUMBLY
- [ ] SKINKY
- [ ] SHARP/TANGY
- [ ] CARAMEL
- [ ] MILKY/LACTIC
- [ ] MOLDY/BLUE
- [ ] LEMON
- [ ] NUTTY
- [ ] BUTTERY/CREAMY
- [ ] EARTHY

MILK
- [ ] COW
- [ ] SHEEP
- [ ] GOAT
- [ ] RAW
- [ ] OTHER: _____

TEXTURE METER
- RUNNY
- SOFT
- SEMI-SOFT
- SEMI-FIRM
- FIRM
- HARD

NOTES
_____
_____
_____
_____
_____
_____

RATING
☆☆☆☆☆

NAME OF CHEESE _____

FACTORY _____

RIND
- ☐ BLOOMY   ☐ WASHED   ☐ NATURAL   ☐ DRY
  - ☐ WHITE   ☐ SALTY   ☐ THICK
  - ☐ SOFT   ☐ HARD
  - ☐ FUZZY   ☐ GRITTY

ORIGIN _____

DATE _____

PRICE _____

FLAVORS
- ☐ SALTY
- ☐ SWEET
- ☐ CRYSTALLINE
- ☐ CRUMBLY
- ☐ SHARP/TANGY
- ☐ MILKY/LACTIC
- ☐ LEMON
- ☐ BUTTERY/CREAMY
- ☐ GRASSY
- ☐ ROBUST
- ☐ HERBAL
- ☐ SKINKY
- ☐ CARAMEL
- ☐ MOLDY/BLUE
- ☐ NUTTY
- ☐ EARTHY

MILK
- ☐ COW
- ☐ SHEEP
- ☐ GOAT
- ☐ RAW
- ☐ OTHER: _____
  _____
  _____

TEXTURE METER
- RUNNY
- SOFT
- SEMI-SOFT
- SEMI-FIRM
- FIRM
- HARD

NOTES
_____
_____
_____
_____
_____
_____

RATING
☆ ☆ ☆ ☆ ☆

NAME OF CHEESE _____

FACTORY _____

RIND
- [ ] BLOOMY
- [ ] WASHED
- [ ] NATURAL
- [ ] DRY
  - [ ] WHITE
  - [ ] SALTY
  - [ ] THICK
  - [ ] SOFT
  - [ ] HARD
  - [ ] FUZZY
  - [ ] GRITTY

ORIGIN _____

DATE _____

PRICE _____

FLAVORS
- [ ] SALTY
- [ ] SWEET
- [ ] CRYSTALLINE
- [ ] CRUMBLY
- [ ] SHARP/TANGY
- [ ] MILKY/LACTIC
- [ ] LEMON
- [ ] BUTTERY/CREAMY
- [ ] GRASSY
- [ ] ROBUST
- [ ] HERBAL
- [ ] SKINKY
- [ ] CARAMEL
- [ ] MOLDY/BLUE
- [ ] NUTTY
- [ ] EARTHY

MILK
- [ ] COW
- [ ] SHEEP
- [ ] GOAT
- [ ] RAW
- [ ] OTHER: _____
  _____
  _____

TEXTURE METER
- RUNNY
- SOFT
- SEMI-SOFT
- SEMI-FIRM
- FIRM
- HARD

NOTES
_____
_____
_____
_____
_____
_____
_____

RATING
☆☆☆☆☆

NAME OF CHEESE _____

FACTORY _____

RIND
- ☐ BLOOMY ☐ WASHED ☐ NATURAL ☐ DRY
  - ☐ WHITE ☐ SALTY ☐ THICK
  - ☐ SOFT ☐ HARD
  - ☐ FUZZY ☐ GRITTY

ORIGIN _____

DATE _____

PRICE _____

FLAVORS
- ☐ SALTY
- ☐ SWEET
- ☐ CRYSTALLINE
- ☐ CRUMBLY
- ☐ SHARP/TANGY
- ☐ MILKY/LACTIC
- ☐ LEMON
- ☐ BUTTERY/CREAMY
- ☐ GRASSY
- ☐ ROBUST
- ☐ HERBAL
- ☐ SKINKY
- ☐ CARAMEL
- ☐ MOLDY/BLUE
- ☐ NUTTY
- ☐ EARTHY

MILK
- ☐ COW
- ☐ SHEEP
- ☐ GOAT
- ☐ RAW
- ☐ OTHER: _____
  _____
  _____

TEXTURE METER
- RUNNY
- SOFT
- SEMI-SOFT
- SEMI-FIRM
- FIRM
- HARD

NOTES
_____
_____
_____
_____
_____

RATING ☆☆☆☆☆

NAME OF CHEESE _____

FACTORY _____

RIND
- [ ] BLOOMY
  - [ ] WHITE
  - [ ] SOFT
  - [ ] FUZZY
- [ ] WASHED
  - [ ] SALTY
- [ ] NATURAL
  - [ ] THICK
  - [ ] HARD
  - [ ] GRITTY
- [ ] DRY

ORIGIN _____

DATE _____

PRICE _____

FLAVORS
- [ ] SALTY
- [ ] SWEET
- [ ] CRYSTALLINE
- [ ] CRUMBLY
- [ ] SHARP/TANGY
- [ ] MILKY/LACTIC
- [ ] LEMON
- [ ] BUTTERY/CREAMY
- [ ] GRASSY
- [ ] ROBUST
- [ ] HERBAL
- [ ] SKINKY
- [ ] CARAMEL
- [ ] MOLDY/BLUE
- [ ] NUTTY
- [ ] EARTHY

MILK
- [ ] COW
- [ ] SHEEP
- [ ] GOAT
- [ ] RAW
- [ ] OTHER: _____
  _____
  _____

TEXTURE METER
- RUNNY
- SOFT
- SEMI-SOFT
- SEMI-FIRM
- FIRM
- HARD

NOTES
_____
_____
_____
_____
_____
_____

RATING ☆☆☆☆☆

NAME OF CHEESE _____

FACTORY _____

RIND
- [ ] BLOOMY
- [ ] WASHED
- [ ] NATURAL
- [ ] DRY
  - [ ] WHITE
  - [ ] SALTY
  - [ ] THICK
  - [ ] SOFT
  - [ ] HARD
  - [ ] FUZZY
  - [ ] GRITTY

ORIGIN _____

DATE _____

PRICE _____

FLAVORS
- [ ] SALTY
- [ ] GRASSY
- [ ] SWEET
- [ ] ROBUST
- [ ] CRYSTALLINE
- [ ] HERBAL
- [ ] CRUMBLY
- [ ] SKINKY
- [ ] SHARP/TANGY
- [ ] CARAMEL
- [ ] MILKY/LACTIC
- [ ] MOLDY/BLUE
- [ ] LEMON
- [ ] NUTTY
- [ ] BUTTERY/CREAMY
- [ ] EARTHY

MILK
- [ ] COW
- [ ] SHEEP
- [ ] GOAT
- [ ] RAW
- [ ] OTHER: _____
  _____
  _____

TEXTURE METER
- RUNNY
- SOFT
- SEMI-SOFT
- SEMI-FIRM
- FIRM
- HARD

NOTES
_____
_____
_____
_____
_____

RATING
☆☆☆☆☆

NAME OF CHEESE _____

FACTORY _____

RIND
- [ ] BLOOMY
- [ ] WASHED
- [ ] NATURAL
- [ ] DRY
  - [ ] WHITE
  - [ ] SALTY
  - [ ] THICK
  - [ ] SOFT
  - [ ] HARD
  - [ ] FUZZY
  - [ ] GRITTY

ORIGIN _____

DATE _____

PRICE _____

FLAVORS
- [ ] SALTY
- [ ] GRASSY
- [ ] SWEET
- [ ] ROBUST
- [ ] CRYSTALLINE
- [ ] HERBAL
- [ ] CRUMBLY
- [ ] SKINKY
- [ ] SHARP/TANGY
- [ ] CARAMEL
- [ ] MILKY/LACTIC
- [ ] MOLDY/BLUE
- [ ] LEMON
- [ ] NUTTY
- [ ] BUTTERY/CREAMY
- [ ] EARTHY

MILK
- [ ] COW
- [ ] SHEEP
- [ ] GOAT
- [ ] RAW
- [ ] OTHER: _____
  _____
  _____

TEXTURE METER
- RUNNY
- SOFT
- SEMI-SOFT
- SEMI-FIRM
- FIRM
- HARD

NOTES
_____
_____
_____
_____
_____
_____

RATING
☆☆☆☆☆

NAME OF CHEESE _____

FACTORY _____

RIND
- ☐ BLOOMY ☐ WASHED ☐ NATURAL ☐ DRY
  - ☐ WHITE   ☐ SALTY   ☐ THICK
  - ☐ SOFT   ☐ HARD
  - ☐ FUZZY   ☐ GRITTY

ORIGIN _____

DATE _____

PRICE _____

FLAVORS
- ☐ SALTY
- ☐ SWEET
- ☐ CRYSTALLINE
- ☐ CRUMBLY
- ☐ SHARP/TANGY
- ☐ MILKY/LACTIC
- ☐ LEMON
- ☐ BUTTERY/CREAMY
- ☐ GRASSY
- ☐ ROBUST
- ☐ HERBAL
- ☐ SKINKY
- ☐ CARAMEL
- ☐ MOLDY/BLUE
- ☐ NUTTY
- ☐ EARTHY

MILK
- ☐ COW
- ☐ SHEEP
- ☐ GOAT
- ☐ RAW
- ☐ OTHER: _____
  _____
  _____

TEXTURE METER
- RUNNY
- SOFT
- SEMI-SOFT
- SEMI-FIRM
- FIRM
- HARD

NOTES
_____
_____
_____
_____
_____

RATING
☆ ☆ ☆ ☆ ☆

NAME OF CHEESE _____

FACTORY _____

RIND
- [ ] BLOOMY
- [ ] WASHED
- [ ] NATURAL
- [ ] DRY
  - [ ] WHITE
  - [ ] SALTY
  - [ ] THICK
  - [ ] SOFT
  - [ ] HARD
  - [ ] FUZZY
  - [ ] GRITTY

ORIGIN _____

DATE _____

PRICE _____

FLAVORS
- [ ] SALTY
- [ ] GRASSY
- [ ] SWEET
- [ ] ROBUST
- [ ] CRYSTALLINE
- [ ] HERBAL
- [ ] CRUMBLY
- [ ] SKINKY
- [ ] SHARP/TANGY
- [ ] CARAMEL
- [ ] MILKY/LACTIC
- [ ] MOLDY/BLUE
- [ ] LEMON
- [ ] NUTTY
- [ ] BUTTERY/CREAMY
- [ ] EARTHY

MILK
- [ ] COW
- [ ] SHEEP
- [ ] GOAT
- [ ] RAW
- [ ] OTHER: _____

TEXTURE METER
- RUNNY
- SOFT
- SEMI-SOFT
- SEMI-FIRM
- FIRM
- HARD

NOTES
_____
_____
_____
_____
_____
_____

RATING
☆☆☆☆☆

NAME OF CHEESE _____

FACTORY _____

RIND
- ☐ BLOOMY ☐ WASHED ☐ NATURAL ☐ DRY
  - ☐ WHITE   ☐ SALTY   ☐ THICK
  - ☐ SOFT   ☐ HARD
  - ☐ FUZZY   ☐ GRITTY

ORIGIN _____

DATE _____

PRICE _____

FLAVORS
- ☐ SALTY
- ☐ SWEET
- ☐ CRYSTALLINE
- ☐ CRUMBLY
- ☐ SHARP/TANGY
- ☐ MILKY/LACTIC
- ☐ LEMON
- ☐ BUTTERY/CREAMY
- ☐ GRASSY
- ☐ ROBUST
- ☐ HERBAL
- ☐ SKINKY
- ☐ CARAMEL
- ☐ MOLDY/BLUE
- ☐ NUTTY
- ☐ EARTHY

MILK
- ☐ COW
- ☐ SHEEP
- ☐ GOAT
- ☐ RAW
- ☐ OTHER: _____
  _____
  _____

TEXTURE METER
- RUNNY
- SOFT
- SEMI-SOFT
- SEMI-FIRM
- FIRM
- HARD

NOTES
_____
_____
_____
_____
_____

RATING
☆☆☆☆☆

NAME OF CHEESE _____

FACTORY _____

RIND
- [ ] BLOOMY [ ] WASHED [ ] NATURAL [ ] DRY
  - [ ] WHITE [ ] SALTY [ ] THICK
  - [ ] SOFT [ ] HARD
  - [ ] FUZZY [ ] GRITTY

ORIGIN _____

DATE _____

PRICE _____

FLAVORS
- [ ] SALTY
- [ ] SWEET
- [ ] CRYSTALLINE
- [ ] CRUMBLY
- [ ] SHARP/TANGY
- [ ] MILKY/LACTIC
- [ ] LEMON
- [ ] BUTTERY/CREAMY
- [ ] GRASSY
- [ ] ROBUST
- [ ] HERBAL
- [ ] SKINKY
- [ ] CARAMEL
- [ ] MOLDY/BLUE
- [ ] NUTTY
- [ ] EARTHY

MILK
- [ ] COW
- [ ] SHEEP
- [ ] GOAT
- [ ] RAW
- [ ] OTHER: _____

TEXTURE METER
- RUNNY
- SOFT
- SEMI-SOFT
- SEMI-FIRM
- FIRM
- HARD

NOTES
_____
_____
_____
_____
_____
_____

RATING
☆☆☆☆☆

NAME OF CHEESE _____

FACTORY _____

RIND

- ☐ BLOOMY ☐ WASHED ☐ NATURAL ☐ DRY
  - ☐ WHITE   ☐ SALTY   ☐ THICK
  - ☐ SOFT   ☐ HARD
  - ☐ FUZZY   ☐ GRITTY

ORIGIN _____

DATE _____

PRICE _____

FLAVORS

- ☐ SALTY   ☐ GRASSY
- ☐ SWEET   ☐ ROBUST
- ☐ CRYSTALLINE   ☐ HERBAL
- ☐ CRUMBLY   ☐ SKINKY
- ☐ SHARP/TANGY   ☐ CARAMEL
- ☐ MILKY/LACTIC   ☐ MOLDY/BLUE
- ☐ LEMON   ☐ NUTTY
- ☐ BUTTERY/CREAMY   ☐ EARTHY

MILK

- ☐ COW
- ☐ SHEEP
- ☐ GOAT
- ☐ RAW
- ☐ OTHER: _____
  _____
  _____

TEXTURE METER

- RUNNY
- SOFT
- SEMI-SOFT
- SEMI-FIRM
- FIRM
- HARD

NOTES

_____
_____
_____
_____
_____
_____

RATING
☆☆☆☆☆

NAME OF CHEESE _____

FACTORY _____

RIND
- ☐ BLOOMY ☐ WASHED ☐ NATURAL ☐ DRY
  - ☐ WHITE ☐ SALTY ☐ THICK
  - ☐ SOFT   ☐ HARD
  - ☐ FUZZY   ☐ GRITTY

ORIGIN _____

DATE _____

PRICE _____

FLAVORS
- ☐ SALTY
- ☐ SWEET
- ☐ CRYSTALLINE
- ☐ CRUMBLY
- ☐ SHARP/TANGY
- ☐ MILKY/LACTIC
- ☐ LEMON
- ☐ BUTTERY/CREAMY
- ☐ GRASSY
- ☐ ROBUST
- ☐ HERBAL
- ☐ SKINKY
- ☐ CARAMEL
- ☐ MOLDY/BLUE
- ☐ NUTTY
- ☐ EARTHY

MILK
- ☐ COW
- ☐ SHEEP
- ☐ GOAT
- ☐ RAW
- ☐ OTHER: _____
  _____
  _____

TEXTURE METER
- RUNNY
- SOFT
- SEMI-SOFT
- SEMI-FIRM
- FIRM
- HARD

NOTES
_____
_____
_____
_____
_____

RATING
☆☆☆☆☆

NAME OF CHEESE _____

FACTORY _____

RIND
- ☐ BLOOMY ☐ WASHED ☐ NATURAL ☐ DRY
  - ☐ WHITE ☐ SALTY ☐ THICK
  - ☐ SOFT ☐ HARD
  - ☐ FUZZY ☐ GRITTY

ORIGIN _____

DATE _____

PRICE _____

FLAVORS
- ☐ SALTY ☐ GRASSY
- ☐ SWEET ☐ ROBUST
- ☐ CRYSTALLINE ☐ HERBAL
- ☐ CRUMBLY ☐ SKINKY
- ☐ SHARP/TANGY ☐ CARAMEL
- ☐ MILKY/LACTIC ☐ MOLDY/BLUE
- ☐ LEMON ☐ NUTTY
- ☐ BUTTERY/CREAMY ☐ EARTHY

MILK
- ☐ COW
- ☐ SHEEP
- ☐ GOAT
- ☐ RAW
- ☐ OTHER: _____
  _____
  _____

TEXTURE METER
- RUNNY
- SOFT
- SEMI-SOFT
- SEMI-FIRM
- FIRM
- HARD

NOTES
_____
_____
_____
_____
_____

RATING
☆ ☆ ☆ ☆ ☆

NAME OF CHEESE _____

FACTORY _____

RIND

- [ ] BLOOMY
- [ ] WASHED
- [ ] NATURAL
- [ ] DRY
  - [ ] WHITE
  - [ ] SOFT
  - [ ] FUZZY
  - [ ] SALTY
  - [ ] THICK
  - [ ] HARD
  - [ ] GRITTY

ORIGIN _____

DATE _____

PRICE _____

FLAVORS

- [ ] SALTY
- [ ] SWEET
- [ ] CRYSTALLINE
- [ ] CRUMBLY
- [ ] SHARP/TANGY
- [ ] MILKY/LACTIC
- [ ] LEMON
- [ ] BUTTERY/CREAMY
- [ ] GRASSY
- [ ] ROBUST
- [ ] HERBAL
- [ ] SKINKY
- [ ] CARAMEL
- [ ] MOLDY/BLUE
- [ ] NUTTY
- [ ] EARTHY

MILK

- [ ] COW
- [ ] SHEEP
- [ ] GOAT
- [ ] RAW
- [ ] OTHER: _____
  _____
  _____

TEXTURE METER

- RUNNY
- SOFT
- SEMI-SOFT
- SEMI-FIRM
- FIRM
- HARD

NOTES

_____
_____
_____
_____
_____
_____

RATING

☆☆☆☆☆

NAME OF CHEESE _____

FACTORY _____

RIND
- ☐ BLOOMY ☐ WASHED ☐ NATURAL ☐ DRY
  - ☐ WHITE ☐ SALTY ☐ THICK
  - ☐ SOFT   ☐ HARD
  - ☐ FUZZY   ☐ GRITTY

ORIGIN _____

DATE _____

PRICE _____

FLAVORS
- ☐ SALTY   ☐ GRASSY
- ☐ SWEET   ☐ ROBUST
- ☐ CRYSTALLINE   ☐ HERBAL
- ☐ CRUMBLY   ☐ SKINKY
- ☐ SHARP/TANGY   ☐ CARAMEL
- ☐ MILKY/LACTIC   ☐ MOLDY/BLUE
- ☐ LEMON   ☐ NUTTY
- ☐ BUTTERY/CREAMY   ☐ EARTHY

MILK
- ☐ COW
- ☐ SHEEP
- ☐ GOAT
- ☐ RAW
- ☐ OTHER: _____
  _____
  _____

TEXTURE METER
- RUNNY
- SOFT
- SEMI-SOFT
- SEMI-FIRM
- FIRM
- HARD

NOTES
_____
_____
_____
_____
_____

RATING
☆☆☆☆☆

NAME OF CHEESE _____

FACTORY _____

RIND
- ☐ BLOOMY ☐ WASHED ☐ NATURAL ☐ DRY
  - ☐ WHITE ☐ SALTY ☐ THICK
  - ☐ SOFT ☐ HARD
  - ☐ FUZZY ☐ GRITTY

ORIGIN _____

DATE _____

PRICE _____

FLAVORS
- ☐ SALTY
- ☐ SWEET
- ☐ CRYSTALLINE
- ☐ CRUMBLY
- ☐ SHARP/TANGY
- ☐ MILKY/LACTIC
- ☐ LEMON
- ☐ BUTTERY/CREAMY
- ☐ GRASSY
- ☐ ROBUST
- ☐ HERBAL
- ☐ SKINKY
- ☐ CARAMEL
- ☐ MOLDY/BLUE
- ☐ NUTTY
- ☐ EARTHY

MILK
- ☐ COW
- ☐ SHEEP
- ☐ GOAT
- ☐ RAW
- ☐ OTHER: _____
  _____
  _____

TEXTURE METER
- RUNNY
- SOFT
- SEMI-SOFT
- SEMI-FIRM
- FIRM
- HARD

NOTES
_____
_____
_____
_____
_____
_____

RATING ☆☆☆☆☆

NAME OF CHEESE _____

FACTORY _____

RIND
- ☐ BLOOMY ☐ WASHED ☐ NATURAL ☐ DRY
  - ☐ WHITE   ☐ SALTY   ☐ THICK
  - ☐ SOFT   ☐ HARD
  - ☐ FUZZY   ☐ GRITTY

ORIGIN _____

DATE _____

PRICE _____

FLAVORS
- ☐ SALTY   ☐ GRASSY
- ☐ SWEET   ☐ ROBUST
- ☐ CRYSTALLINE   ☐ HERBAL
- ☐ CRUMBLY   ☐ SKINKY
- ☐ SHARP/TANGY   ☐ CARAMEL
- ☐ MILKY/LACTIC   ☐ MOLDY/BLUE
- ☐ LEMON   ☐ NUTTY
- ☐ BUTTERY/CREAMY ☐ EARTHY

MILK
- ☐ COW
- ☐ SHEEP
- ☐ GOAT
- ☐ RAW
- ☐ OTHER: _____
  _____
  _____

TEXTURE METER
- RUNNY
- SOFT
- SEMI-SOFT
- SEMI-FIRM
- FIRM
- HARD

NOTES
_____
_____
_____
_____
_____
_____

RATING
☆ ☆ ☆ ☆ ☆

NAME OF CHEESE _____

FACTORY _____

RIND
- [ ] BLOOMY
- [ ] WASHED
- [ ] NATURAL
- [ ] DRY
  - [ ] WHITE
  - [ ] SOFT
  - [ ] FUZZY
  - [ ] SALTY
  - [ ] THICK
  - [ ] HARD
  - [ ] GRITTY

ORIGIN _____

DATE _____

PRICE _____

FLAVORS
- [ ] SALTY
- [ ] SWEET
- [ ] CRYSTALLINE
- [ ] CRUMBLY
- [ ] SHARP/TANGY
- [ ] MILKY/LACTIC
- [ ] LEMON
- [ ] BUTTERY/CREAMY
- [ ] GRASSY
- [ ] ROBUST
- [ ] HERBAL
- [ ] SKINKY
- [ ] CARAMEL
- [ ] MOLDY/BLUE
- [ ] NUTTY
- [ ] EARTHY

MILK
- [ ] COW
- [ ] SHEEP
- [ ] GOAT
- [ ] RAW
- [ ] OTHER: _____
  _____
  _____

TEXTURE METER
- RUNNY
- SOFT
- SEMI-SOFT
- SEMI-FIRM
- FIRM
- HARD

NOTES
_____
_____
_____
_____
_____
_____

RATING
☆☆☆☆☆

NAME OF CHEESE _____

FACTORY _____

RIND

- ☐ BLOOMY ☐ WASHED ☐ NATURAL ☐ DRY
  - ☐ WHITE ☐ SALTY ☐ THICK
  - ☐ SOFT ☐ HARD
  - ☐ FUZZY ☐ GRITTY

ORIGIN _____

DATE _____

PRICE _____

FLAVORS

- ☐ SALTY ☐ GRASSY
- ☐ SWEET ☐ ROBUST
- ☐ CRYSTALLINE ☐ HERBAL
- ☐ CRUMBLY ☐ SKINKY
- ☐ SHARP/TANGY ☐ CARAMEL
- ☐ MILKY/LACTIC ☐ MOLDY/BLUE
- ☐ LEMON ☐ NUTTY
- ☐ BUTTERY/CREAMY ☐ EARTHY

MILK

- ☐ COW
- ☐ SHEEP
- ☐ GOAT
- ☐ RAW
- ☐ OTHER: _____
  _____
  _____

TEXTURE METER

- RUNNY
- SOFT
- SEMI-SOFT
- SEMI-FIRM
- FIRM
- HARD

NOTES

_____
_____
_____
_____
_____
_____

RATING ☆☆☆☆☆

NAME OF CHEESE _____

FACTORY _____

RIND
- ☐ BLOOMY ☐ WASHED ☐ NATURAL ☐ DRY
  - ☐ WHITE   ☐ SALTY   ☐ THICK
  - ☐ SOFT   ☐ HARD
  - ☐ FUZZY   ☐ GRITTY

ORIGIN _____

DATE _____

PRICE _____

FLAVORS
- ☐ SALTY
- ☐ SWEET
- ☐ CRYSTALLINE
- ☐ CRUMBLY
- ☐ SHARP/TANGY
- ☐ MILKY/LACTIC
- ☐ LEMON
- ☐ BUTTERY/CREAMY
- ☐ GRASSY
- ☐ ROBUST
- ☐ HERBAL
- ☐ SKINKY
- ☐ CARAMEL
- ☐ MOLDY/BLUE
- ☐ NUTTY
- ☐ EARTHY

MILK
- ☐ COW
- ☐ SHEEP
- ☐ GOAT
- ☐ RAW
- ☐ OTHER: _____
  _____
  _____

TEXTURE METER
- RUNNY
- SOFT
- SEMI-SOFT
- SEMI-FIRM
- FIRM
- HARD

NOTES
_____
_____
_____
_____
_____
_____
_____

RATING ☆☆☆☆☆

NAME OF CHEESE _____

FACTORY _____

RIND
- ☐ BLOOMY ☐ WASHED ☐ NATURAL ☐ DRY
  - ☐ WHITE ☐ SALTY ☐ THICK
  - ☐ SOFT ☐ HARD
  - ☐ FUZZY ☐ GRITTY

ORIGIN _____

DATE _____

PRICE _____

FLAVORS
- ☐ SALTY ☐ GRASSY
- ☐ SWEET ☐ ROBUST
- ☐ CRYSTALLINE ☐ HERBAL
- ☐ CRUMBLY ☐ SKINKY
- ☐ SHARP/TANGY ☐ CARAMEL
- ☐ MILKY/LACTIC ☐ MOLDY/BLUE
- ☐ LEMON ☐ NUTTY
- ☐ BUTTERY/CREAMY ☐ EARTHY

MILK
- ☐ COW
- ☐ SHEEP
- ☐ GOAT
- ☐ RAW
- ☐ OTHER: _____
  _____
  _____

TEXTURE METER
- RUNNY
- SOFT
- SEMI-SOFT
- SEMI-FIRM
- FIRM
- HARD

NOTES
_____
_____
_____
_____
_____
_____

RATING
☆ ☆ ☆ ☆ ☆

NAME OF CHEESE _____

FACTORY _____

RIND

- [ ] BLOOMY
- [ ] WASHED
- [ ] NATURAL
- [ ] DRY
  - [ ] WHITE
  - [ ] SALTY
  - [ ] THICK
  - [ ] SOFT
  - [ ] HARD
  - [ ] FUZZY
  - [ ] GRITTY

ORIGIN _____

DATE _____

PRICE _____

FLAVORS

- [ ] SALTY
- [ ] GRASSY
- [ ] SWEET
- [ ] ROBUST
- [ ] CRYSTALLINE
- [ ] HERBAL
- [ ] CRUMBLY
- [ ] SKINKY
- [ ] SHARP/TANGY
- [ ] CARAMEL
- [ ] MILKY/LACTIC
- [ ] MOLDY/BLUE
- [ ] LEMON
- [ ] NUTTY
- [ ] BUTTERY/CREAMY
- [ ] EARTHY

MILK

- [ ] COW
- [ ] SHEEP
- [ ] GOAT
- [ ] RAW
- [ ] OTHER: _____

TEXTURE METER

- RUNNY
- SOFT
- SEMI-SOFT
- SEMI-FIRM
- FIRM
- HARD

NOTES

_____
_____
_____
_____
_____
_____

RATING

☆☆☆☆☆

NAME OF CHEESE _____

FACTORY _____

RIND
- [ ] BLOOMY
- [ ] WASHED
- [ ] NATURAL
- [ ] DRY
  - [ ] WHITE
  - [ ] SALTY
  - [ ] THICK
  - [ ] SOFT
  - [ ] HARD
  - [ ] FUZZY
  - [ ] GRITTY

ORIGIN _____

DATE _____

PRICE _____

FLAVORS
- [ ] SALTY
- [ ] GRASSY
- [ ] SWEET
- [ ] ROBUST
- [ ] CRYSTALLINE
- [ ] HERBAL
- [ ] CRUMBLY
- [ ] SKINKY
- [ ] SHARP/TANGY
- [ ] CARAMEL
- [ ] MILKY/LACTIC
- [ ] MOLDY/BLUE
- [ ] LEMON
- [ ] NUTTY
- [ ] BUTTERY/CREAMY
- [ ] EARTHY

MILK
- [ ] COW
- [ ] SHEEP
- [ ] GOAT
- [ ] RAW
- [ ] OTHER: _____
  _____
  _____

TEXTURE METER
- RUNNY
- SOFT
- SEMI-SOFT
- SEMI-FIRM
- FIRM
- HARD

NOTES
_____
_____
_____
_____
_____

RATING ☆☆☆☆☆

NAME OF CHEESE _____

FACTORY _____

RIND
- [ ] BLOOMY
- [ ] WASHED
- [ ] NATURAL
- [ ] DRY
  - [ ] WHITE
  - [ ] SALTY
  - [ ] THICK
  - [ ] SOFT
  - [ ] HARD
  - [ ] FUZZY
  - [ ] GRITTY

ORIGIN _____

DATE _____

PRICE _____

FLAVORS
- [ ] SALTY
- [ ] GRASSY
- [ ] SWEET
- [ ] ROBUST
- [ ] CRYSTALLINE
- [ ] HERBAL
- [ ] CRUMBLY
- [ ] SKINKY
- [ ] SHARP/TANGY
- [ ] CARAMEL
- [ ] MILKY/LACTIC
- [ ] MOLDY/BLUE
- [ ] LEMON
- [ ] NUTTY
- [ ] BUTTERY/CREAMY
- [ ] EARTHY

MILK
- [ ] COW
- [ ] SHEEP
- [ ] GOAT
- [ ] RAW
- [ ] OTHER: _____

TEXTURE METER
- RUNNY
- SOFT
- SEMI-SOFT
- SEMI-FIRM
- FIRM
- HARD

NOTES
_____
_____
_____
_____
_____
_____

RATING
☆☆☆☆☆

NAME OF CHEESE _____

FACTORY _____

RIND

- [ ] BLOOMY [ ] WASHED [ ] NATURAL [ ] DRY
  - [ ] WHITE [ ] SALTY [ ] THICK
  - [ ] SOFT   [ ] HARD
  - [ ] FUZZY   [ ] GRITTY

ORIGIN _____

DATE _____

PRICE _____

FLAVORS

- [ ] SALTY
- [ ] SWEET
- [ ] CRYSTALLINE
- [ ] CRUMBLY
- [ ] SHARP/TANGY
- [ ] MILKY/LACTIC
- [ ] LEMON
- [ ] BUTTERY/CREAMY
- [ ] GRASSY
- [ ] ROBUST
- [ ] HERBAL
- [ ] SKINKY
- [ ] CARAMEL
- [ ] MOLDY/BLUE
- [ ] NUTTY
- [ ] EARTHY

MILK

- [ ] COW
- [ ] SHEEP
- [ ] GOAT
- [ ] RAW
- [ ] OTHER: _____
  _____
  _____

TEXTURE METER

- RUNNY
- SOFT
- SEMI-SOFT
- SEMI-FIRM
- FIRM
- HARD

NOTES

_____
_____
_____
_____
_____

RATING ☆☆☆☆☆

NAME OF CHEESE _____

FACTORY _____

RIND

- [ ] BLOOMY
- [ ] WASHED
- [ ] NATURAL
- [ ] DRY
  - [ ] WHITE
  - [ ] SOFT
  - [ ] FUZZY
  - [ ] SALTY
  - [ ] THICK
  - [ ] HARD
  - [ ] GRITTY

ORIGIN _____

DATE _____

PRICE _____

FLAVORS

- [ ] SALTY
- [ ] SWEET
- [ ] CRYSTALLINE
- [ ] CRUMBLY
- [ ] SHARP/TANGY
- [ ] MILKY/LACTIC
- [ ] LEMON
- [ ] BUTTERY/CREAMY
- [ ] GRASSY
- [ ] ROBUST
- [ ] HERBAL
- [ ] SKINKY
- [ ] CARAMEL
- [ ] MOLDY/BLUE
- [ ] NUTTY
- [ ] EARTHY

MILK

- [ ] COW
- [ ] SHEEP
- [ ] GOAT
- [ ] RAW
- [ ] OTHER: _____
  _____
  _____

TEXTURE METER

- RUNNY
- SOFT
- SEMI-SOFT
- SEMI-FIRM
- FIRM
- HARD

NOTES

_____
_____
_____
_____
_____
_____

RATING

☆☆☆☆☆

NAME OF CHEESE _____

FACTORY _____

RIND
- ☐ BLOOMY ☐ WASHED ☐ NATURAL ☐ DRY
  - ☐ WHITE ☐ SALTY ☐ THICK
  - ☐ SOFT ☐ HARD
  - ☐ FUZZY ☐ GRITTY

ORIGIN _____

DATE _____

PRICE _____

FLAVORS
- ☐ SALTY
- ☐ SWEET
- ☐ CRYSTALLINE
- ☐ CRUMBLY
- ☐ SHARP/TANGY
- ☐ MILKY/LACTIC
- ☐ LEMON
- ☐ BUTTERY/CREAMY
- ☐ GRASSY
- ☐ ROBUST
- ☐ HERBAL
- ☐ SKINKY
- ☐ CARAMEL
- ☐ MOLDY/BLUE
- ☐ NUTTY
- ☐ EARTHY

MILK
- ☐ COW
- ☐ SHEEP
- ☐ GOAT
- ☐ RAW
- ☐ OTHER: _____
  _____
  _____

TEXTURE METER
- RUNNY
- SOFT
- SEMI-SOFT
- SEMI-FIRM
- FIRM
- HARD

NOTES
_____
_____
_____
_____
_____
_____

RATING ☆☆☆☆☆

NAME OF CHEESE _____

FACTORY _____

RIND
- ☐ BLOOMY ☐ WASHED ☐ NATURAL ☐ DRY
  - ☐ WHITE ☐ SALTY ☐ THICK
  - ☐ SOFT ☐ HARD
  - ☐ FUZZY ☐ GRITTY

ORIGIN _____

DATE _____

PRICE _____

FLAVORS
- ☐ SALTY
- ☐ SWEET
- ☐ CRYSTALLINE
- ☐ CRUMBLY
- ☐ SHARP/TANGY
- ☐ MILKY/LACTIC
- ☐ LEMON
- ☐ BUTTERY/CREAMY
- ☐ GRASSY
- ☐ ROBUST
- ☐ HERBAL
- ☐ SKINKY
- ☐ CARAMEL
- ☐ MOLDY/BLUE
- ☐ NUTTY
- ☐ EARTHY

MILK
- ☐ COW
- ☐ SHEEP
- ☐ GOAT
- ☐ RAW
- ☐ OTHER: _____
  _____
  _____

TEXTURE METER
- RUNNY
- SOFT
- SEMI-SOFT
- SEMI-FIRM
- FIRM
- HARD

NOTES
_____
_____
_____
_____
_____
_____

RATING ☆☆☆☆☆

NAME OF CHEESE _____

FACTORY _____

RIND
- ☐ BLOOMY ☐ WASHED ☐ NATURAL ☐ DRY
  - ☐ WHITE   ☐ SALTY   ☐ THICK
  - ☐ SOFT   ☐ HARD
  - ☐ FUZZY   ☐ GRITTY

ORIGIN _____

DATE _____

PRICE _____

FLAVORS
- ☐ SALTY
- ☐ SWEET
- ☐ CRYSTALLINE
- ☐ CRUMBLY
- ☐ SHARP/TANGY
- ☐ MILKY/LACTIC
- ☐ LEMON
- ☐ BUTTERY/CREAMY
- ☐ GRASSY
- ☐ ROBUST
- ☐ HERBAL
- ☐ SKINKY
- ☐ CARAMEL
- ☐ MOLDY/BLUE
- ☐ NUTTY
- ☐ EARTHY

MILK
- ☐ COW
- ☐ SHEEP
- ☐ GOAT
- ☐ RAW
- ☐ OTHER: _____
  _____
  _____

TEXTURE METER
- RUNNY
- SOFT
- SEMI-SOFT
- SEMI-FIRM
- FIRM
- HARD

NOTES
_____
_____
_____
_____
_____
_____

RATING ☆☆☆☆☆

NAME OF CHEESE _____

FACTORY _____

RIND

- [ ] BLOOMY [ ] WASHED [ ] NATURAL [ ] DRY
  - [ ] WHITE [ ] SALTY [ ] THICK
  - [ ] SOFT [ ] HARD
  - [ ] FUZZY [ ] GRITTY

ORIGIN _____

DATE _____

PRICE _____

FLAVORS

- [ ] SALTY
- [ ] SWEET
- [ ] CRYSTALLINE
- [ ] CRUMBLY
- [ ] SHARP/TANGY
- [ ] MILKY/LACTIC
- [ ] LEMON
- [ ] BUTTERY/CREAMY
- [ ] GRASSY
- [ ] ROBUST
- [ ] HERBAL
- [ ] SKINKY
- [ ] CARAMEL
- [ ] MOLDY/BLUE
- [ ] NUTTY
- [ ] EARTHY

MILK

- [ ] COW
- [ ] SHEEP
- [ ] GOAT
- [ ] RAW
- [ ] OTHER: _____ _____ _____

TEXTURE METER

- RUNNY
- SOFT
- SEMI-SOFT
- SEMI-FIRM
- FIRM
- HARD

NOTES

_____
_____
_____
_____
_____
_____
_____

RATING ☆☆☆☆☆

NAME OF CHEESE _____

FACTORY _____

RIND
- ☐ BLOOMY ☐ WASHED ☐ NATURAL ☐ DRY
  - ☐ WHITE ☐ SALTY ☐ THICK
  - ☐ SOFT ☐ HARD
  - ☐ FUZZY ☐ GRITTY

ORIGIN _____

DATE _____

PRICE _____

FLAVORS
- ☐ SALTY ☐ GRASSY
- ☐ SWEET ☐ ROBUST
- ☐ CRYSTALLINE ☐ HERBAL
- ☐ CRUMBLY ☐ SKINKY
- ☐ SHARP/TANGY ☐ CARAMEL
- ☐ MILKY/LACTIC ☐ MOLDY/BLUE
- ☐ LEMON ☐ NUTTY
- ☐ BUTTERY/CREAMY ☐ EARTHY

MILK
- ☐ COW
- ☐ SHEEP
- ☐ GOAT
- ☐ RAW
- ☐ OTHER: _____
  _____
  _____

TEXTURE METER
- RUNNY
- SOFT
- SEMI-SOFT
- SEMI-FIRM
- FIRM
- HARD

NOTES
_____
_____
_____
_____
_____
_____

RATING ☆☆☆☆☆

NAME OF CHEESE _____

FACTORY _____

RIND

- ☐ BLOOMY ☐ WASHED ☐ NATURAL ☐ DRY
  - ☐ WHITE   ☐ SALTY   ☐ THICK
  - ☐ SOFT   ☐ HARD
  - ☐ FUZZY   ☐ GRITTY

ORIGIN _____

DATE _____

PRICE _____

FLAVORS

- ☐ SALTY
- ☐ SWEET
- ☐ CRYSTALLINE
- ☐ CRUMBLY
- ☐ SHARP/TANGY
- ☐ MILKY/LACTIC
- ☐ LEMON
- ☐ BUTTERY/CREAMY
- ☐ GRASSY
- ☐ ROBUST
- ☐ HERBAL
- ☐ SKINKY
- ☐ CARAMEL
- ☐ MOLDY/BLUE
- ☐ NUTTY
- ☐ EARTHY

MILK

- ☐ COW
- ☐ SHEEP
- ☐ GOAT
- ☐ RAW
- ☐ OTHER:
  _____
  _____
  _____

TEXTURE METER

- RUNNY
- SOFT
- SEMI-SOFT
- SEMI-FIRM
- FIRM
- HARD

NOTES

_____
_____
_____
_____
_____
_____

RATING ☆☆☆☆☆

NAME OF CHEESE _____

FACTORY _____

RIND
- ☐ BLOOMY ☐ WASHED ☐ NATURAL ☐ DRY
  - ☐ WHITE   ☐ SALTY   ☐ THICK
  - ☐ SOFT   ☐ HARD
  - ☐ FUZZY   ☐ GRITTY

ORIGIN _____

DATE _____

PRICE _____

FLAVORS
- ☐ SALTY
- ☐ SWEET
- ☐ CRYSTALLINE
- ☐ CRUMBLY
- ☐ SHARP/TANGY
- ☐ MILKY/LACTIC
- ☐ LEMON
- ☐ BUTTERY/CREAMY
- ☐ GRASSY
- ☐ ROBUST
- ☐ HERBAL
- ☐ SKINKY
- ☐ CARAMEL
- ☐ MOLDY/BLUE
- ☐ NUTTY
- ☐ EARTHY

MILK
- ☐ COW
- ☐ SHEEP
- ☐ GOAT
- ☐ RAW
- ☐ OTHER: _____
  _____
  _____

TEXTURE METER
- RUNNY
- SOFT
- SEMI-SOFT
- SEMI-FIRM
- FIRM
- HARD

NOTES
_____
_____
_____
_____
_____
_____

RATING
☆ ☆ ☆ ☆ ☆

NAME OF CHEESE _____

FACTORY _____

RIND

- [ ] BLOOMY - [ ] WASHED - [ ] NATURAL - [ ] DRY
  - [ ] WHITE
  - [ ] SOFT
  - [ ] FUZZY
  - [ ] SALTY
  - [ ] THICK
  - [ ] HARD
  - [ ] GRITTY

ORIGIN _____

DATE _____

PRICE _____

FLAVORS

- [ ] SALTY
- [ ] SWEET
- [ ] CRYSTALLINE
- [ ] CRUMBLY
- [ ] SHARP/TANGY
- [ ] MILKY/LACTIC
- [ ] LEMON
- [ ] BUTTERY/CREAMY
- [ ] GRASSY
- [ ] ROBUST
- [ ] HERBAL
- [ ] SKINKY
- [ ] CARAMEL
- [ ] MOLDY/BLUE
- [ ] NUTTY
- [ ] EARTHY

MILK

- [ ] COW
- [ ] SHEEP
- [ ] GOAT
- [ ] RAW
- [ ] OTHER: _____
  _____
  _____

TEXTURE METER

- RUNNY
- SOFT
- SEMI-SOFT
- SEMI-FIRM
- FIRM
- HARD

NOTES

_____
_____
_____
_____
_____
_____

RATING ☆☆☆☆☆

NAME OF CHEESE _____

FACTORY _____

RIND
- [ ] BLOOMY   [ ] WASHED   [ ] NATURAL   [ ] DRY
  - [ ] WHITE   [ ] SALTY   [ ] THICK
  - [ ] SOFT   [ ] HARD
  - [ ] FUZZY   [ ] GRITTY

ORIGIN _____

DATE _____

PRICE _____

FLAVORS
- [ ] SALTY
- [ ] SWEET
- [ ] CRYSTALLINE
- [ ] CRUMBLY
- [ ] SHARP/TANGY
- [ ] MILKY/LACTIC
- [ ] LEMON
- [ ] BUTTERY/CREAMY
- [ ] GRASSY
- [ ] ROBUST
- [ ] HERBAL
- [ ] SKINKY
- [ ] CARAMEL
- [ ] MOLDY/BLUE
- [ ] NUTTY
- [ ] EARTHY

MILK
- [ ] COW
- [ ] SHEEP
- [ ] GOAT
- [ ] RAW
- [ ] OTHER: _____
  _____
  _____

TEXTURE METER
- RUNNY
- SOFT
- SEMI-SOFT
- SEMI-FIRM
- FIRM
- HARD

NOTES
_____
_____
_____
_____
_____
_____

RATING ☆☆☆☆☆

NAME OF CHEESE _____

FACTORY _____

RIND
- [ ] BLOOMY
  - [ ] WHITE
  - [ ] SOFT
  - [ ] FUZZY
- [ ] WASHED
  - [ ] SALTY
- [ ] NATURAL
  - [ ] THICK
  - [ ] HARD
  - [ ] GRITTY
- [ ] DRY

ORIGIN _____

DATE _____

PRICE _____

FLAVORS
- [ ] SALTY
- [ ] SWEET
- [ ] CRYSTALLINE
- [ ] CRUMBLY
- [ ] SHARP/TANGY
- [ ] MILKY/LACTIC
- [ ] LEMON
- [ ] BUTTERY/CREAMY
- [ ] GRASSY
- [ ] ROBUST
- [ ] HERBAL
- [ ] SKINKY
- [ ] CARAMEL
- [ ] MOLDY/BLUE
- [ ] NUTTY
- [ ] EARTHY

MILK
- [ ] COW
- [ ] SHEEP
- [ ] GOAT
- [ ] RAW
- [ ] OTHER: _____
  _____
  _____

TEXTURE METER
- RUNNY
- SOFT
- SEMI-SOFT
- SEMI-FIRM
- FIRM
- HARD

NOTES
_____
_____
_____
_____
_____
_____

RATING ☆☆☆☆☆

NAME OF CHEESE _____

FACTORY _____

RIND
- [ ] BLOOMY [ ] WASHED [ ] NATURAL [ ] DRY
  - [ ] WHITE [ ] SALTY [ ] THICK
  - [ ] SOFT   [ ] HARD
  - [ ] FUZZY   [ ] GRITTY

ORIGIN _____

DATE _____

PRICE _____

FLAVORS
- [ ] SALTY
- [ ] SWEET
- [ ] CRYSTALLINE
- [ ] CRUMBLY
- [ ] SHARP/TANGY
- [ ] MILKY/LACTIC
- [ ] LEMON
- [ ] BUTTERY/CREAMY
- [ ] GRASSY
- [ ] ROBUST
- [ ] HERBAL
- [ ] SKINKY
- [ ] CARAMEL
- [ ] MOLDY/BLUE
- [ ] NUTTY
- [ ] EARTHY

MILK
- [ ] COW
- [ ] SHEEP
- [ ] GOAT
- [ ] RAW
- [ ] OTHER: _____
  _____
  _____

TEXTURE METER
- RUNNY
- SOFT
- SEMI-SOFT
- SEMI-FIRM
- FIRM
- HARD

NOTES
_____
_____
_____
_____
_____
_____

RATING
☆ ☆ ☆ ☆ ☆

NAME OF CHEESE _____

FACTORY _____

RIND

- [ ] BLOOMY
- [ ] WASHED
- [ ] NATURAL
- [ ] DRY
  - [ ] WHITE
  - [ ] SOFT
  - [ ] FUZZY
  - [ ] SALTY
  - [ ] THICK
  - [ ] HARD
  - [ ] GRITTY

ORIGIN _____

DATE _____

PRICE _____

FLAVORS

- [ ] SALTY
- [ ] SWEET
- [ ] CRYSTALLINE
- [ ] CRUMBLY
- [ ] SHARP/TANGY
- [ ] MILKY/LACTIC
- [ ] LEMON
- [ ] BUTTERY/CREAMY
- [ ] GRASSY
- [ ] ROBUST
- [ ] HERBAL
- [ ] SKINKY
- [ ] CARAMEL
- [ ] MOLDY/BLUE
- [ ] NUTTY
- [ ] EARTHY

MILK

- [ ] COW
- [ ] SHEEP
- [ ] GOAT
- [ ] RAW
- [ ] OTHER: _____

TEXTURE METER

- RUNNY
- SOFT
- SEMI-SOFT
- SEMI-FIRM
- FIRM
- HARD

NOTES

_____
_____
_____
_____
_____
_____

RATING ☆☆☆☆☆

NAME OF CHEESE _____

FACTORY _____

RIND
- ☐ BLOOMY   ☐ WASHED   ☐ NATURAL   ☐ DRY
  - ☐ WHITE   ☐ SALTY   ☐ THICK
  - ☐ SOFT   ☐ HARD
  - ☐ FUZZY   ☐ GRITTY

ORIGIN _____

DATE _____

PRICE _____

FLAVORS
- ☐ SALTY   ☐ GRASSY
- ☐ SWEET   ☐ ROBUST
- ☐ CRYSTALLINE   ☐ HERBAL
- ☐ CRUMBLY   ☐ SKINKY
- ☐ SHARP/TANGY   ☐ CARAMEL
- ☐ MILKY/LACTIC   ☐ MOLDY/BLUE
- ☐ LEMON   ☐ NUTTY
- ☐ BUTTERY/CREAMY   ☐ EARTHY

MILK
- ☐ COW
- ☐ SHEEP
- ☐ GOAT
- ☐ RAW
- ☐ OTHER: _____
  _____
  _____

TEXTURE METER
- RUNNY
- SOFT
- SEMI-SOFT
- SEMI-FIRM
- FIRM
- HARD

NOTES
_____
_____
_____
_____
_____
_____

RATING
☆☆☆☆☆

NAME OF CHEESE _____

FACTORY _____

RIND
- ☐ BLOOMY ☐ WASHED ☐ NATURAL ☐ DRY
  - ☐ WHITE   ☐ SALTY   ☐ THICK
  - ☐ SOFT   ☐ HARD
  - ☐ FUZZY   ☐ GRITTY

ORIGIN _____

DATE _____

PRICE _____

FLAVORS
- ☐ SALTY
- ☐ SWEET
- ☐ CRYSTALLINE
- ☐ CRUMBLY
- ☐ SHARP/TANGY
- ☐ MILKY/LACTIC
- ☐ LEMON
- ☐ BUTTERY/CREAMY
- ☐ GRASSY
- ☐ ROBUST
- ☐ HERBAL
- ☐ SKINKY
- ☐ CARAMEL
- ☐ MOLDY/BLUE
- ☐ NUTTY
- ☐ EARTHY

MILK
- ☐ COW
- ☐ SHEEP
- ☐ GOAT
- ☐ RAW
- ☐ OTHER: _____
  _____
  _____

TEXTURE METER
- RUNNY
- SOFT
- SEMI-SOFT
- SEMI-FIRM
- FIRM
- HARD

NOTES
_____
_____
_____
_____
_____
_____

RATING ☆☆☆☆☆

NAME OF CHEESE _____

FACTORY _____

RIND
- ☐ BLOOMY ☐ WASHED ☐ NATURAL ☐ DRY
  - ☐ WHITE   ☐ SALTY   ☐ THICK
  - ☐ SOFT   ☐ HARD
  - ☐ FUZZY   ☐ GRITTY

ORIGIN _____

DATE _____

PRICE _____

FLAVORS
- ☐ SALTY   ☐ GRASSY
- ☐ SWEET   ☐ ROBUST
- ☐ CRYSTALLINE   ☐ HERBAL
- ☐ CRUMBLY   ☐ SKINKY
- ☐ SHARP/TANGY   ☐ CARAMEL
- ☐ MILKY/LACTIC ☐ MOLDY/BLUE
- ☐ LEMON   ☐ NUTTY
- ☐ BUTTERY/CREAMY ☐ EARTHY

MILK
- ☐ COW
- ☐ SHEEP
- ☐ GOAT
- ☐ RAW
- ☐ OTHER: _____
  _____
  _____

TEXTURE METER
- RUNNY
- SOFT
- SEMI-SOFT
- SEMI-FIRM
- FIRM
- HARD

NOTES
_____
_____
_____
_____
_____
_____

RATING ☆☆☆☆☆

www.ingramcontent.com/pod-product-compliance
Lightning Source LLC
Chambersburg PA
CBHW081231080526
44587CB00022B/3902